Christmas Season Prayer Book

The Twelve days of Christmas

Copyright © 2015, 2020 by Daniel D. Schroeder

All rights reserved. No part of this book may be reproduced, stored in a retrieval system, or transmitted in any form or by any means, electronic, mechanical, including photocopying, recording, or otherwise, without the written permission of the copyright holder.

The Scripture quotations contained herein are from the New Revised Standard Version of the Bible, copyright © 1989 by the Division of Christian Education of the National Council of the Churches of Christ in the U.S.A., and are used by permission. All rights reserved.

First Edition, April 2015

Printed in the United States of America

ISBN   978-0-692-39933-0

The Twelve Days of Christmas

Other related books...

Reclaiming Eden

Reclaiming Your Soul

Holy Week Prayer Book

A Common Rule for Monastics

Living Waters from the Well

Common Rule Prayer Book

For God so loved the world that He gave us His only begotten Son, that whoever believes in him shall not perish, but have eternal life.

Introduction

The Community of the Gospel was formed as a response to the Great Commandments: "You shall love the Lord your God with all your heart, and with all your soul, and with all your mind." And, "You shall love your neighbor as yourself."

We are a non-residential Monastic Community whose members try to help each other on their spiritual journeys. We do this by living a monastic life of daily prayer, reflective study, and personal service while remaining in the secular world. We seek to demonstrate our faith in unique ways as best we can, while allowing our lives to be transformed by God.

Our Community is…

Gospel-centered - The core of our being comes from the teaching and grace of the Living Word. We hope to be examples of the Gospel message. Our strength and healing power comes from the knowledge of the Gospel - we are a group of like-minded people seeking the love of Christ that transcends our shortcomings and those of the world around us. We continue to grow and learn together, finding the way to His Truth.

Ecumenical - Although based in the Episcopal Church, we welcome any Christian seeker who shares our values and desires to fully know, love, and serve the Lord.

Faith-based - We know that we are saved through faith, but we demonstrate our faith through actively practicing monastic principles of prayer, study and service in unique ways.

Inclusive - acceptance into the Community is based on one's desire to share in the treasures of love and compassion of Our Lord. It is not based on age, gender, marital status, sexual orientation, academic achievement or ethnicity.

Non-residential - Our members live and work in various places, but are connected by the love and wisdom of Christ. Our spiritual home is in the heart of Christ.

Contemplative and Action-oriented - we strive to blend the contemplative life with a life of action in a spirit of collaboration. The contemplative life gives us the strength, wisdom and desire to use our talents and abilities in the world, and the world of action provides us with material for further prayer and contemplation.

Although we are primarily a dispersed community (we live and work in various parts of the world), we travel together as one in spirit with Our Lord. We believe that our purpose is to awaken to God's wisdom and love, and to shape our lives following God's principles. The expression of our personal mission in life is a response to the love of God who made each of us in a unique way. We join together as the body of Christ to share our journey and our resources as we are able, and to mutually encourage each other's faith journey.

The Charism of this Community is to live the monastic vows of Daily Prayer, Reflective Study and Personal Service that lead to nurturing of the soul at the hands and heart of Christ. This results in our knowing, loving and serving the Lord in our own unique way, as God made us.

Members become transformed by living what we value. Not that these things in themselves do the transforming, but they put us in a position whereby we can be transformed by the love of God.

Our Core Vows...

For thousands of years people have been striving to open the pathways of life to receive the enduring love of God. Frequently, these pathways rest in devotion, knowledge, and action. The vows we hold dearest reflect these three ancient, sacred pathways. They are the foundation of our monastic practice; this is what we do and who we are.

Prayer is how we express the Way of Devotion. We view this vow to mean spending time daily in the presence of God during prayer and meditation. Our Members will usually pray 1 to 4 times daily, using a format that suits their individual prayer temperament. Our prayer time is "spiritual breathing." It is a time when we take in His love and compassion for us and for the world, and then share this with others through thanksgiving, praise, intercessions and supplications.

While we have several Community Prayer Books, members are encouraged to explore Prayer Books in a variety of formats. This particular Prayer Book guides the participant through Morning and Evening Prayer for the Twelve Days of Christmas. (It's assumed that corporate worship would be used for the Sunday services.)
The next page provides some suggestions for using this Prayer Book.

Blessings to you on your journey!

Concerning the Christmas Season Office

Prayer time is like a good meal, so don't rush through it. Say them slowly and savor them. Leave silence (30 seconds or so) between parts or where silence is indicated.

It is suggested that you offer your prayers following a 15-20 minute Centering Prayer/Presence. This will help prepare your mind and spirit for the service.

Sunday Mass takes precedence over Morning Prayer.

Some readings from the Gospel are compilations of multiple Gospels as their scripture provides.

The rubrics for standing and sitting are optional, and depend on whether the prayer is being offered by an individual or a small group.

When candles are used, whenever possible, they should be lit by a female, signifying that the Blessed Virgin Mary brought the Light into the world.

Additional Collects and prayers may be added as desired.

Neck crosses, prayer shawls and stoles may be worn at any time by anyone offering the prayers.

Noonday prayer and Compline may be offered using another suitable format.

December 25
Nativity of Our Lord

That Jesus was born is a fact both of history and revelation. The precise date of his birth, however, is not recorded in the Gospels, which are, after all, not biographies, and show little concern for those biographical details. It was in Rome, in 336, that the date, December 25, was settled upon for the celebration of the Nativity. The day was already a sacred one coming as it does at the winter solstice. The observance spread rapidly throughout the West; and it is accepted by many of the Eastern Churches. The full title of the feast dates from the 1662edition of the Book of Common Prayer, The word "Christmas" is a contraction of "Christ's Mass."

EVENING PRAYER

I. Invitatory

The officiant opens with this sentence: (All stand)

"For God so loved the world that he gave his only begotten Son, that whosoever believeth in him should not perish, but have everlasting life." (John 3:16)

O God, make speed to save us.
O Lord, make haste to help us.

Glory to the Father, and to the Son,
and to the Holy Spirit. *
**As it was in the beginning, is now,
and will be for ever. Amen.**

December 25

Phos Hilaron

O gracious Light, pure brightness of the ever-living Father in heaven, *
O Jesus Christ, holy and blessed!

Now as we have come to the setting of the sun, and our eyes behold the vesper light, *
We sing your praises, O God: Father, Son and Holy Spirit.

You are worthy at all times to be praised by happy voices, O Son of God, O Giver of life, *
And to be glorified through all the worlds.

Psalm (*Psalm 110*)

The Father loves the Son, *
And has given all things into His hand.

The Lord said to my Lord, "Sit at my right hand, *
    Until I make your enemies your footstool."
The Lord will send the scepter of your power out of Zion, *
    Saying, "Rule over your enemies round about you.
Princely state has been yours from the day of your birth; *
    In the beauty of holiness have I begotten you
    like dew from the womb of the morning."
The Lord has sworn and he will not recant: *
    "You are a priest for ever after the order of
    Melchizedek."
The Lord who is at your right hand will smite kings in the day of his victory; *
    He will rule over the nations.

Glory to the Father, and to the Son,
and to the Holy Spirit. *
As it was in the beginning, is now,
and will be for ever. Amen.

The Father loves the Son, *
And has given all things into His hand.

II. The Lessons *(Be seated)*

Old Testament Lesson

A reading from the Book of Micah (4 & 5)

Now it shall come to pass in the latter days that the mountain of the Lord's house shall be established on the top of the mountains, and shall be exalted above the hills; and people shall flow to it.
    Many nations shall come and say, "Come, and let us go up to the mountain of the Lord, to the house of the God of Jacob; he will teach us his ways, and we shall walk in his paths.
    For out of Zion the law shall go forth, and the Word of the Lord from Jerusalem. He shall discern between many peoples, and rebuke strong nations from afar; they shall beat their swords into plowshares, and their spears into pruning hooks.
    Nation shall not lift up sword against nation; neither shall they learn war anymore. But everyone shall sit under his vine and under his fig tree, and no one shall make them afraid; for the mouth of the Lord of hosts has spoken. For all people will walk in the name of the Lord our God forever and ever.

December 25

But you, Bethlehem, though you are little among the thousands in Judah, out of you shall come forth the One to be Ruler of Israel, whose goings forth are from of old, from everlasting. And he shall stand and feed his flock in the strength of the Lord; and this One shall be peace.

The Word of the Lord.

Silence for reflection.

Canticle (The Prologue of John)

In the beginning was the Word,
    And the Word was with God.
And the Word was God,
    He was in the beginning with God.
All things were made through him,
    And without him was not anything made that was made.
In him was life,
    And the life was the light of the human race.
The light shines in the darkness,
    And the darkness has never overcome it.
He was in the world, and the world was made through him,
    Yet the world knew him not.
He came to his own home,
    And his own people would not receive him.
But to all who received him, who believed on his name,
    He has given power to become children of God.
They were born not of blood, nor of the will of the flesh,
    Nor of any human will, but of God.
And the Word became flesh,
    And dwelt among us, full of grace and truth.
We have seen his glory,
    Glory as of the only Son from the Father.
And from his fullness we have all received,
    Even grace upon grace.

Reading of the Gospel *(All stand)*

The Holy Gospel of Our Lord Jesus Christ according to John (3:31-36)

He who comes from above is above all; he who is of the world is worldly and speaks of the world. He who comes from heaven is above all. And what he has seen and heard, that is what he testifies; but few receive his testimony. He who has received his testimony knows that God is true. For he whom God has sent speaks the words of God, for God does not withhold the Spirit from him. The Father loves the Son, and has given all things into His hand. He who believes in the Son has everlasting life; and he who does not believe the Son cannot see life, but lives in darkness.

The Gospel of the Lord.
Praise be to You, O Christ. *(Be seated)*

Silence for reflection, homily or reading.

[Jesus came to earth to teach us how to live with mercy, compassion and love. How can we all make sure our thoughts, words, and deeds reflect this?]

Magnificat

My soul proclaims the greatness of the Lord*
    My spirit rejoices in God my Savior.
You have looked with favor on your humble servant*
    And all generations will call me blessed.
You, O God, have done great things for me*
    And holy is your name.
You have mercy on those who love you*
    From generation to generation.
You have shown the strength of your arm*
    And have scattered the proud in their conceit.
You have cast down the mighty from their thrones*
    And have lifted up the lowly,
You have filled the hungry with good things*
    And the rich you have sent away empty.
You have come to the help of your people*
    For you remembered your promise of mercy.
The promise you made to our forbears*
    To Abraham and his children forever.

Lord, O Gracious Light.
Christ, O Compassionate Love.
Lord, O Gracious Light.

Rejoice! Rejoice!
Emmanuel shall come to you, O Israel.

Hymn   "O Come, O Come Emmanuel"

III. The Prayers

The Lord be with you.
And also with you.

The Lord's Prayer *(Stand facing altar)*

Our Father in heaven, hallowed be your name,
    Your kingdom come, your will be done,
    On earth as it is in heaven.
Give us today our daily bread.
Forgive us, as we forgive others.
Save us from the time of trial and deliver us from evil.
For the kingdom, the power, and the glory are yours
    Now and forever. Amen

Collect

O God, you make us glad by the yearly festival of the birth of your Son Jesus Christ: Grant that we, who joyfully receive him as our Redeemer, may with sure confidence behold him when he comes to be our Healer; who lives and reigns with you and the Holy Spirit, one God, now and for ever. Amen.

Additional Prayers may be added here.

May the Lord bless us, keep us from evil, and lead us to eternal life. **Amen.**

Let us bless the Lord.
Thanks be to God.

December 26
St. Stephen, Deacon & Martyr

Probably a Hellenistic Jew, Stephen was one of the "seven men of good repute, full of the Spirit of wisdom," (Acts 6:3) who were chosen by the apostles to relieve them of the administrative burden of "serving tables and caring for the widows." By this appointment to assist the Apostles, Stephen became the first to do what the Church traditionally considers to be the work and ministry of a deacon. Stephen also preached and performed many miracles. Eventually he was accused of blasphemy by the Jewish leaders, and brought before the Sanhedrin where he preached a sermon. He was dragged out of the city and stoned to death.

MORNING PRAYER

I. Invitatory

The officiant opens with this sentence (All stand)

Jesus Christ is born! *
Glory to God in the highest!

Come Emmanuel!   **God with us!**

O Lord, Open our lips. *
And our mouth shall proclaim Your praise.

Glory to the Father, and to the Son,
and to the Holy Spirit. *
**As it was in the beginning, is now,
and will be for ever. Amen.**

December 26

Psalm   *Psalm 30*

In the beginning was the Word, *
And the Word was with God, and the Word was God.

I will extol you, O Lord, for you have lifted me up, *
    And have not let my foes rejoice over me.
O Lord, my God, I cried out to you, *
    And you healed me.
O Lord, you brought my soul up from the grave; *
    You have kept me alive, to avoid the pit.
Sing praise to the Lord, you saints of his, *
    And give thanks in remembrance of his Holy
    Name.
For his anger is but for a moment, *
    His favor is for life.
Weeping may endure for a night, *
    But joy comes in the morning.
You have turned for me my mourning
into dancing, *
    You have put off my sackcloth
    And clothed me with gladness.
May my glory sing praise to you and not be silent, *
    O Lord my God, I will give thanks to you for ever.

Glory to the Father, and to the Son,
and to the Holy Spirit. *
**As it was in the beginning, is now,
and will be for ever. Amen.**

In the beginning was the Word, *
And the Word was with God, and the Word was God.

II. The Lessons *(Be seated)*

Old Testament Lesson

A reading from the book of 2 Chronicles (24:17-21)

Now after the death of Jehoiada the leaders of Judah came and bowed down to the king. And the king listened to them. Because of this, they abandoned the house of the Lord God of their fathers, and served wooden images and idols; and wrath came upon Judah and Jerusalem. Yet, God sent prophets to them, to bring them back to the Lord; and the prophets testified against them, but they would not listen. Then the Spirit of God came to Zechariah, son of the priest, who said to the people, "Thus says God: 'Why do you transgress my commandments so that you cannot prosper? Because you have forsaken the Lord, he cannot help you.'" So the people conspired against him, and at the command of the king they stoned him in the court of the house of the Lord.

The word of the Lord.

Silence for reflection.

December 26

Canticle

It came upon the midnight clear,
That glorious song of old,
From angels bending near the earth,
To touch their harps of gold!
Peace on the earth, good will to men,
From heaven's all gracious King!
The world in solemn stillness lay,
To hear the angels sing.

Still through the cloven skies they come,
With peaceful wings unfurled,
And still their heavenly music floats,
Over all the weary world;
Above its sad and lowly plains,
They bend on hovering wing.
And ever over its Babel sounds,
The blessed angels sing.

Yet with the woes of sin and strife,
The world has suffered long;
Beneath the angel-strain have rolled,
Two thousand years of wrong;
And man, at war with man, hears not,
The love song which they bring:
O hush the noise, you men of strife,
And hear the angels sing.

December 26

New Testament Lesson

A reading from the Book of Acts (6:8-15, 58-60)

Stephen, full of grace and power, did great wonders and signs among the people. Then some of those who belonged to the synagogue of the Freedmen, Cyrenians, Alexandrians, and others of those from Cilicia and Asia, stood up and argued with Stephen. But they could not withstand the wisdom and the Spirit with which he spoke. Then they secretly instigated some men to say, "We have heard him speak blasphemous words against Moses and God. They stirred up the people as well as the elders and the scribes; then they suddenly confronted him, seized him, and brought him before the council. They set up false witnesses who said, "This man never stops saying things against this holy place and the law; for we have heard him say that this Jesus will destroy this place and will change the customs that Moses handed on to us." And all who sat in the council looked intently at him, and they saw that his face was like the face of an angel. Then they dragged him out of the city and began to stone him. Then he knelt down and cried out in a loud voice, "Lord, do not hold this sin against them." When he had said this, he died.

The word of the Lord.

Silence for reflection, homily or reading.

[Why are those who try to follow God's way sometimes persecuted?]

December 26

Benedictus

Blessed are you O Lord our God*
    You have come to your people and set them free.
You have raised up for us a mighty Savior*
    Born of the house of your servant David.
Through your holy prophets you promised of old*
    That you would save us from our enemies,
    From the hands of all who hate us.
You promised to show mercy to our forbears*
    And to remember your holy covenant.
This was the oath you swore to our father Abraham*
    To set us free from the hands of our enemies,
Free to worship you without fear*
    Holy and righteous in your sight all the days of our life.
And you, child, shall be called the prophet of the Most High*
    For you will go before the Lord to prepare the way,
To give God's people knowledge of salvation*
    Through the forgiveness of their sins.
In the tender compassion of our God*
    The dawn from on high shall break upon us.
To shine on those who dwell in darkness and the shadow of death*
    And to guide our feet into the way of peace.

Glory to the Father, and to the Son,
and to the Holy Spirit. *
**As it was in the beginning, is now,
and will be for ever. Amen.**

Peace on the earth, good will to men,
From heaven's all gracious King!

Hymn (It Came Upon a Midnight Clear)

III. The Prayers

The Lord be with you all.
And also with you.

The Lord's Prayer *(Stand facing altar)*

Our Father in heaven, hallowed be your name,
    Your kingdom come, your will be done,
    On earth as it is in heaven.
Give us today our daily bread.
Forgive us, as we forgive others.
Save us from the time of trial and deliver us from evil.
For the kingdom, the power, and the glory are yours
    Now and forever. Amen

Collect

We give you thanks, O Lord of glory, for the example of the first martyr Stephen, who looked up to heaven and prayed for his persecutors to your Son Jesus Christ, who stands at your right hand; where he lives and reigns with you and the Holy Spirit, one God, in glory everlasting.

Additional Prayers may be added here.

The grace of Our Lord Jesus Christ, and the love of God, and the companionship of the Holy Spirit, be in us and those absent from us. **Amen.**

Let us bless the Lord. **Thanks be to God.**

December 26

EVENING PRAYER

I. Invitatory

The officiant opens with this sentence: (All stand)

All the generations from Abraham to David are fourteen generations;
And from David to the exile in Babylon are fourteen generations;
And from the exile to the Messiah are fourteen generations.

O God, make speed to save us.
O Lord, make haste to help us.

Glory to the Father, and to the Son,
and to the Holy Spirit. *
**As it was in the beginning, is now,
and will be for ever. Amen.**

Phos Hilaron

O gracious Light, pure brightness of the ever-living Father in heaven, *
O Jesus Christ, holy and blessed!

Now as we have come to the setting of the sun, and our eyes behold the vesper light, *
We sing your praises, O God: Father, Son and Holy Spirit.

You are worthy at all times to be praised by happy voices, O Son of God, O Giver of life, *
And to be glorified through all the worlds.

Psalm *(Be seated)*

This is the day the Lord has made; *
Let us rejoice and be glad in it.

from Psalm 118

O give thanks to the Lord, for he is good; *
    His steadfast love endures forever!
With the Lord at my side I do not fear. *
    What can mortals do to me?
The Lord is my strength and my might; *
    He has become my salvation.
There are songs of victory in the tents of the righteous; *
    The right hand of the Lord does valiantly;
I shall not die, but I shall live, *
    And recount the deeds of the Lord.
The stone that the builders rejected *
    Has become the chief cornerstone.
This is the Lord's doing; *
    It is marvelous in our eyes.
This is the day the Lord has made; *
    Let us rejoice and be glad in it.
Blessed is he who comes in the name of the Lord. *
    We bless you from the house of the Lord.
The Lord is God, and he has given us the Light. *
    Bind the festal procession with branches!
O give thanks to the Lord, for he is good, *
    For his steadfast love endures forever.

Glory to the Father, and to the Son,
and to the Holy Spirit. *
**As it was in the beginning, is now,
and will be for ever. Amen.**

This is the day the Lord has made; *
    Let us rejoice and be glad in it.

II. The Lessons

First Reading of the Gospel *(All stand)*

The Holy Gospel of Our Lord Jesus Christ according to Matthew (10:16-20)

"See, I am sending you out like sheep into the midst of wolves; so be wise as serpents and innocent as doves. Beware of them, for they will hand you over to councils and flog you in their synagogues; and you will be dragged before governors and kings because of me, as a testimony to them and the Gentiles. When they hand you over, do not worry about what to say; for what you are to say will be given to you at that time; for it is not you who speak, but the Spirit of your Father speaking through you."

The Gospel of the Lord.
Praise be to You, O Christ. *(Be seated)*

Silence for reflection, homily or reading.

December 26

Canticle

I heard the bells on Christmas day
Their old familiar carols play,
And wild and sweet the words repeat
Of peace on earth, good will to men.

I thought how, as the day had come,
The belfries of all Christendom
Had rolled along the unbroken song
Of peace on earth, good will to men.

And in despair I bowed my head
There is no peace on earth, I said,
For hate is strong and mocks the song
Of peace on earth, good will to men.

Then pealed the bells more loud and deep:
God is not dead, nor doth He sleep;
The wrong shall fail, the right prevail
With peace on earth, good will to men.

Till ringing, singing on its way
The world revolved from night to day,
A voice, a chime, a chant sublime
Of peace on earth, good will to men.

Second Reading of the Gospel *(All stand)*

The Holy Gospel of Our Lord Jesus Christ according to Matthew (23:34-37)

Therefore I send you prophets, sages, and scribes, some of whom you will kill and crucify, and some you will flog in your synagogues and pursue from town to town, so that upon you may come all the righteous blood shed on earth. Jerusalem, Jerusalem, the city that kills the prophets and stones those who are sent to it! How often have I desired to gather your children together as a hen gathers her brood under her wings, and you were not willing!

The Gospel of the Lord.
Praise be to You, O Christ.

Be seated. Silence for reflection, homily or reading.

[What does it mean to you to "be wise as serpents, but innocent as doves"?]

December 26

Magnificat

My soul proclaims the greatness of the Lord*
    My spirit rejoices in God my Savior.
You have looked with favor on your humble servant*
    And all generations will call me blessed.
You, O God, have done great things for me*
    And holy is your name.
You have mercy on those who love you*
    From generation to generation.
You have shown the strength of your arm*
    And have scattered the proud in their conceit.
You have cast down the mighty from their thrones*
    And have lifted up the lowly,
You have filled the hungry with good things*
    And the rich you have sent away empty.
You have come to the help of your people*
    For you remembered your promise of mercy.
The promise you made to our forbears*
    To Abraham and his children forever.

Lord, O Gracious Light!
Christ, O Perfect Love!
Lord, O Gracious Light!

Hymn (I Heard the Bells on Christmas Day)

III. The Prayers

The Lord be with you.
And also with you.

The Lord's Prayer *(Stand facing altar)*

Our Father in heaven, hallowed be your name,
    Your kingdom come, your will be done,
    On earth as it is in heaven.
Give us today our daily bread.
Forgive us, as we forgive others.
Save us from the time of trial and deliver us from evil.
For the kingdom, the power, and the glory are yours
    Now and forever. Amen

Collect

Almighty God, you have poured upon us the new Light of your incarnate Word: Grant that this Light, enkindled in our hearts, may shine forth in our lives; through Jesus Christ our Lord, who lives and reigns with you, in the unity of the Holy Spirit, one God, now and forever. **Amen.**

Additional Prayers may be added here.

May the Lord bless us, keep us from evil, and lead us to eternal life. **Amen.**

Let us bless the Lord.   **Thanks be to God.**

December 27
St. John, Apostle & Evangelist

John, the son of Zebedee, with his brother James, was called from being a fisherman to be a disciple and a "fisher of men." He became one of the inner group of three disciples whom Jesus chose to be with him at the raising of Jairus' daughter, at the Transfiguration, and in the garden of Gethsemane. If John is to be identified with the "disciple whom Jesus loved," then he clearly enjoyed a very special relationship with his Master, reclining close to Jesus at the Last Supper, receiving the care of his mother at the cross, and being the first to understand the truth of the empty tomb. According to tradition, John was eventually exiled to the island of Patmos where he experienced visions recounted in the Book of Revelation.

December 27

MORNING PRAYER

I. Invitatory

The officiant opens with this sentence: (All stand)

All things came into being through him, *
And without him not one thing came into being.

O Lord, Open our lips. *
And our mouth shall proclaim Your praise.

Glory to the Father, and to the Son,
and to the Holy Spirit. *
**As it was in the beginning, is now,
and will be for ever. Amen.**

Psalm

Joy to the world, the Lord is come;
Let earth receive her King!

from Psalm 98

O sing to the Lord a new song, *
    For he has done marvelous things.
His right hand and his holy arm *
    Have gotten him victory.
The Lord has made known his victory; *
    He has revealed his vindication
    in the sight of the nations.

December 27

He has remembered his steadfast love and
faithfulness to the house of Israel, *
> All ends of the earth have seen the victory of our
> God.

Make a joyful noise to the Lord all the earth; *
> Break forth into joyous song and sing praises.

Sing praises to the Lord with the lyre, *
> With the lyre and the sound of melody.

With trumpets and the sound of the horn *
> Make a joyful noise before the King, the Lord.

Let the sea roar, and all that fills it; *
> The world and those who live in it.

Let the waters claps their hands; *
Let the hills sing together for joy.
Sing for joy at the presence of the Lord, *
> For the Lord is coming to rule the earth.

He will rule the world with righteousness, *
And the people with equity.

Glory to the Father, and to the Son,
and to the Holy Spirit. *
**As it was in the beginning, is now,
and will be for ever. Amen.**

Joy to the world, the Lord is come;
Let earth receive her King!

December 27

II. The Lessons *(Be seated)*

Old Testament Lesson

A reading from the book of Proverbs (8:22-30)

    The Lord created me at the beginning of his work, the first of his acts long ago. Ages ago I was set up, at the first, before the beginning of the earth. When there were no depths I was brought forth, when there were no springs abounding with water. Before the mountains had been shaped, before the hills, I was brought forth – when he had not yet made earth and fields, or the world's first bits of soil.
    When he established the heavens, I was there, when he drew a circle on the face of the deep, when he made firm the skies above, when he established the fountains of the deep, when he assigned to the sea its limit, so that the waters might not transgress his command, when he marked out the foundations of the earth, then I was beside him, like a master worker; and I was daily his delight, rejoicing before him always.

The word of the Lord.

Silence for reflection.

Canticle

Joy to the world, the Lord is come;
Let earth receive her King;
Let every heart prepare Him room,
And heaven and nature sing.

Joy to the earth, the Savior reigns;
Let men their songs employ;
While fields and floods,
Rocks, hills and plains
Repeat the sounding joy.

He rules the world with truth and grace,
And makes the nations prove
The glories of His righteousness,
And wonders of His love.

New Testament Lesson

A reading from the Book of 1 John (1:1-7)

We declare to you what was from the beginning, what we have heard, what we have seen with our eyes, what we have looked at and touched with our hands, concerning the Word of life – this life was revealed, and we have seen it and testify to it, and declare to you the eternal life that was with the Father and was revealed to us – we declare to you what we have seen and heard so that you also may have fellowship with us; and truly our fellowship is with the Father and with his Son Jesus Christ.

We are writing these things so that our joy may be complete. This is the message we have heard from him and proclaim to you, that God is light and in him there is no darkness at all. If we say that we have fellowship with him while we are walking in darkness, we lie and do not do what is true; but if we walk in the light as he himself is in the light, we have fellowship with one another.

The word of the Lord.

Silence for reflection, homily or reading.

[What does the "Light" mean to you? What does "darkness" mean to you?]

Benedictus

Blessed are you O Lord our God*
    You have come to your people and set them free.
You have raised up for us a mighty Savior*
    Born of the house of your servant David.
Through your holy prophets you promised of old*
    That you would save us from our enemies,
    From the hands of all who hate us.
You promised to show mercy to our forbears*
    And to remember your holy covenant.
This was the oath you swore to our father Abraham*
    To set us free from the hands of our enemies,
Free to worship you without fear*

> Holy and righteous in your sight all the days of our life.

And you, child, shall be called the prophet of the Most High*
> For you will go before the Lord to prepare the way,

To give God's people knowledge of salvation*
> Through the forgiveness of their sins.

In the tender compassion of our God*
> The dawn from on high shall break upon us.

To shine on those who dwell in darkness and the shadow of death*
> And to guide our feet into the way of peace.

Glory to the Father, and to the Son,
and to the Holy Spirit. *
**As it was in the beginning, is now,
and will be for ever. Amen.**

Let every heart prepare Him room,
And heaven and nature sing!

Hymn (Joy to the World)

III. The Prayers

The Lord be with you all.
And also with you.

The Lord's Prayer   *(Stand facing altar)*

Our Father in heaven, hallowed be your name,
    Your kingdom come, your will be done,
    On earth as it is in heaven.
Give us today our daily bread.
Forgive us, as we forgive others.
Save us from the time of trial and deliver us from evil.
For the kingdom, the power, and the glory are yours
    Now and forever. Amen

Collect

Shed upon your Church, O Lord, the brightness of your Light, that we, being illuminated by the teaching of your apostle and evangelist John, may so walk in the Light of your truth, that at length we may attain to the fullness of eternal life; through Jesus Christ our Lord, who lives and reigns with you and the Holy Spirit, one God, for ever and ever, Amen.

Additional Prayers may be added here.

The grace of Our Lord Jesus Christ, and the love of God, and the companionship of the Holy Spirit, be in us and those absent from us.   **Amen.**

Let us bless the Lord.   **Thanks be to God.**

December 27

EVENING PRAYER

I. Invitatory

The officiant opens with this sentence: (All stand)

Jesus Christ is born! *
Glory to God in the highest!

O God, make speed to save us.
O Lord, make haste to help us.

Glory to the Father, and to the Son,
and to the Holy Spirit. *
**As it was in the beginning, is now,
and will be for ever. Amen.**

Phos Hilaron

O gracious Light, pure brightness of the ever-living Father in heaven, *
O Jesus Christ, holy and blessed!

Now as we have come to the setting of the sun, and our eyes behold the vesper light, *
We sing your praises, O God: Father, Son and Holy Spirit.

You are worthy at all times to be praised by happy voices, O Son of God, O Giver of life, *
And to be glorified through all the worlds.

December 27

Psalm

Come and behold him, *
Born the King of angels.

Psalm 145(1-9)

I will extol you, my God and my King, *
    And bless your name forever.
Every day I will bless you, *
    And praise your name for ever.
Great is the Lord, and greatly to be praised; *
    His greatness is unsurpassed.
One generation shall praise your works to another, *
    And shall declare your mighty deeds.
On the glorious splendor of your majesty, *
    And on your wondrous works I will meditate.
The might of your awesome deeds shall be proclaimed, *
    and I will declare your greatness.
They shall celebrate the fame of your abundant goodness, *
    And shall sing aloud of your righteousness.
The Lord is gracious and merciful, *
    Slow to anger and abounding in steadfast love.
The Lord is good to all, *
    And his compassion is over all that he has made.

Glory to the Father, and to the Son,
and to the Holy Spirit. *
**As it was in the beginning, is now,
and will be for ever. Amen.**

Come and behold him, *
Born the King of angels.

II. The Lessons *(Be seated)*

Old Testament Lesson

A reading from the Book of Isaiah (44:1-8)

But now hear, O Jacob my servant, Israel whom I have chosen! Thus says the Lord who made you, who formed you in the womb and will help you: Do not fear O Jacob my servant, Jeshurun whom I have chosen. For I will pour water on the thirsty land, and streams on the dry ground; I will pour my Spirit upon your descendants, and my blessing on your offspring. They will spring up like a green tamarisk, like willows by flowing streams. This one will say, "I am the Lord's," another will be called by the name of Jacob, yet another will write on the hand, "The Lord's," and adopt the name of Israel. Thus says the Lord, the King of Israel, and his Redeemer, the Lord of hosts; I am the first and the last; besides me there is no god. Who is like me? Let them proclaim it, let them declare and set it forth before me. Who has announced from of old the things to come? Let them tell us what is yet to be. Do not fear, or be afraid; have I not told you from of old and declared it? You are my witnesses. Is there any god besides me? There is no other rock; I know not one.

The Word of the Lord.

Silence for reflection.

December 27

Canticle

O come, all ye faithful,
Joyful and triumphant,
O come ye, O come ye to Bethlehem;
Come and behold him,
Born the King of angels;
O Come, let us adore him, Christ the Lord.

God of God, Light of Light,
Lo! he abhors not the Virgin's womb:
Very God, Begotten, not created;

Sing, choirs of angels,
Sing in exultation,
Sing, all ye citizens of heaven above;
Glory to God In the highest;

See how the shepherds,
Summoned to his cradle,
Leaving their flocks, draw nigh to gaze;
We too will thither
Bend our joyful footsteps;

Yea, Lord, we greet thee,
Born this happy morning;
Jesus, to thee be glory given;
Word of the Father,
Now in flesh appearing.

Reading of the Gospel *(All stand)*

The Holy Gospel of Our Lord Jesus Christ according to John (1:29-34)

The next day [John the Baptist] saw Jesus coming toward him and declared, "Here is the Lamb of God who takes away the sin of the world! This is he of whom I said, 'After me comes a man who ranks ahead of me because he was before me.' I myself did not know him; but I came baptizing with water for this reason, that he might be revealed to Israel."

And John testified, "I saw the Spirit descending from heaven like a dove, and it remained on him. I myself did not know him, but the one who sent me to baptize with water said to me, 'He on whom you see the Spirit descend and remain is the one who baptizes with the Holy Spirit.' And I myself have seen and have testified that this is the Son of God.

The Gospel of the Lord.
Praise be to You, O Christ.

Silence for reflection, homily or reading. Be seated.

[Our baptismal vows ask us to work toward justice, peace and dignity of all persons. What does that mean to you in your life?]

December 27

Magnificat

My soul proclaims the greatness of the Lord*
    My spirit rejoices in God my Savior.
You have looked with favor on your humble servant*
    And all generations will call me blessed.
You, O God, have done great things for me*
    And holy is your name.
You have mercy on those who love you*
    From generation to generation.
You have shown the strength of your arm*
    And have scattered the proud in their conceit.
You have cast down the mighty from their thrones*
    And have lifted up the lowly,
You have filled the hungry with good things*
    And the rich you have sent away empty.
You have come to the help of your people*
    For you remembered your promise of mercy.
The promise you made to our forbears*
    To Abraham and his children forever.

Lord, O Gracious Light!
Christ, O Perfect Love!
Lord, O Gracious Light!

Hymn (O Come, All Ye Faithful)

December 27

III. The Prayers

The Lord be with you.
And also with you.

The Lord's Prayer *(Stand facing altar)*

Our Father in heaven, hallowed be your name,
    Your kingdom come, your will be done,
    On earth as it is in heaven.
Give us today our daily bread.
Forgive us, as we forgive others.
Save us from the time of trial and deliver us from evil.
For the kingdom, the power, and the glory are yours
    Now and forever. Amen

Collect

Almighty God, by our baptism into the death and resurrection of your Son Jesus Christ, you turn us from the old life of darkness to a new life of Light; Grant that we, being reborn to this new life in him, may live in his love all our days, seeking justice, peace, and the dignity of all persons, through Jesus Christ our Lord, who lives and reigns with you and the Holy Spirit, one God, now and forever. Amen.

Additional Prayers may be added here.

May the Lord bless us, keep us from evil, and lead us to eternal life. **Amen.**

Let us bless the Lord. **Thanks be to God.**

December 28
The Holy Innocents

Herod the Great, ruler of the Jews, appointed by the Romans in 40 B.C., kept peace in Palestine for 37 years. His ruthless control, coupled with genuine ability, has been recorded by the Jewish historian Josephus, who describes him as "a man of great barbarity toward everyone." He was continually in fear of losing his throne. It is not surprising that the Wise Men's report of the birth of an infant King of the Jews (Matthew 2) caused him fear and anger. To protect himself against this infant king, Herod ordered the slaughter of all male children less than two years of age in Bethlehem and the surrounding region.

MORNING PRAYER

I. Invitatory

The officiant opens with this sentence: (All stand)

Jesus Christ is born! *
Glory to God in the highest!

Come Emmanuel!
God with us!

O Lord, Open our lips. *
And our mouth shall proclaim Your praise.

December 28

Psalm   *(Psalm 2)*

O star of wonder, star of night, *
Guide us to Thy perfect light.

Why do the nations conspire, *
    And the people plot in vain?
The kings of the earth set themselves, *
    And the rulers take counsel together,
Against the Lord and his anointed, saying *
    "Let us burst their bonds asunder,
    and cast their cords from us."
He who sits in heaven laughs; *
    The Lord has them in derision.
Then he will speak to them in his wrath, *
    And terrify them in his fury, saying,
I have set my king on Zion, *
    My holy hill.
I will tell you of the decree of the Lord; *
    "You are my son; today I have begotten you.
Ask of me, and I will make the nations your heritage, *
    And the ends of the earth your possession.
You shall break them with a rod of iron, *
    And dash them in pieces like a potter's vessel.
Now therefore, O kings, be wise; *
    Be warned, O rulers of the earth.
Serve the Lord with awe, *
    With humility kiss his feet,
Or his anger will stir, and your way will vanish. *
    Happy are they who take refuge in him.

Glory to the Father, and to the Son,
and to the Holy Spirit. *
As it was in the beginning, is now,
and will be for ever. Amen.

O star of wonder, star of night, *
Guide us to Thy perfect light.

II. The Lessons *(Be seated)*

Old Testament Lesson

A reading from the book of Jeremiah (31:15-17)

    Thus says the Lord; A voice is heard in Ramah, lamentation and bitter weeping. Rachel is weeping for her children; she refuses to be comforted for her children, because they are no more.
    Thus says the Lord: Keep your voice from weeping, and your eyes from tears; for there is a reward for your work.
    Thus says the Lord: They shall come back from the land of the enemy; there is hope for your future.
    Thus says the Lord: Your children shall come back to their own country.

The word of the Lord.

Silence for reflection.

December 28

Canticle

We three kings of Orient are
Bearing gifts, we traverse afar.
Field and fountain, moor and mountain,
Following yonder star.

Born a King on Bethlehem plain,
Gold I bring to crown Him again,
King forever, Ceasing never
Over us all to reign.

Glorious now behold Him arise,
King and God and sacrifice.
Heav'n sings Hallelujah;
Hallelujah the earth replies.

O star of wonder, star of night,
Star with royal beauty bright,
Westward leading, still proceeding,
Guide us to Thy perfect light.

December 28

New Testament Lesson

A reading from the Book of Revelation (21:1-6)

    Then I saw a new heaven and a new earth; for the first heaven and the first earth had passed away, and the sea was no more. And I saw the holy city, the new Jerusalem, coming down out of heaven from God, prepared as a bride adorned for her husband. And I heard a loud voice from the throne saying, "See, the home of God is among mortals. He will dwell with them; they will be his people, and God himself will be with them; he will wipe away every tear from their eyes. Death will be no more; mourning and crying and pain will be no more, for the first things have passed away."
    And the one who was seated on the throne said, "See, I am making all things new." Also he said, "Write this, for these words are trustworthy and true." Then he said to me, "It is done! I am the Alpha and the Omega, the beginning and the end. To the thirsty I will give water as a gift from the spring of the water of life."

The word of the Lord.

Silence for reflection, homily or reading

[How has the coming of Christ created a new earth for you?]

December 28

Benedictus

Blessed are you O Lord our God*
> You have come to your people and set them free.

You have raised up for us a mighty Savior*
> Born of the house of your servant David.

Through your holy prophets you promised of old*
> That you would save us from our enemies,
> From the hands of all who hate us.

You promised to show mercy to our forbears*
> And to remember your holy covenant.

This was the oath you swore to our father Abraham*
> To set us free from the hands of our enemies,

Free to worship you without fear*
> Holy and righteous in your sight all the days of our life.

And you, child, shall be called the prophet of the Most High*
> For you will go before the Lord to prepare the way,

To give God's people knowledge of salvation*
> Through the forgiveness of their sins.

In the tender compassion of our God*
> The dawn from on high shall break upon us.

To shine on those who dwell in darkness and the shadow of death*
> And to guide our feet into the way of peace.

Glory to the Father, and to the Son,
and to the Holy Spirit. *
**As it was in the beginning, is now,
and will be for ever. Amen.**

Prayer and praising, All men raising, *
Worship Him God on high.

December 28

Hymn   (We Three Kings of Orient Are)

III. The Prayers

The Lord be with you all.
And also with you.

The Lord's Prayer   *(Stand facing altar)*

Our Father in heaven, hallowed be your name,
    Your kingdom come, your will be done,
    On earth as it is in heaven.
Give us today our daily bread.
Forgive us, as we forgive others.
Save us from the time of trial and deliver us from evil.
For the kingdom, the power, and the glory are yours
    Now and forever. Amen

Collect

We remember today, O God, the slaughter of the holy innocents of Bethlehem by King Herod. Receive, we pray, into the arms of your mercy all innocent victims; and by your great might frustrate the designs of evil tyrants and establish your role of justice, love, and peace; through Jesus Christ our Lord, who lives and reigns with you, in the unity of the Holy Spirit, one God, forever and ever. **Amen.**

Additional Prayers may be added here.

December 28

The grace of Our Lord Jesus Christ, and the love of God, and the companionship of the Holy Spirit, be in us and those absent from us.
Amen.

Let us bless the Lord.
Thanks be to God.

December 28

EVENING PRAYER

I. Invitatory

The officiant opens with this sentence: (All stand)

O God, make speed to save us.
O Lord, make haste to help us.

Glory to the Father, and to the Son,
and to the Holy Spirit. *
**As it was in the beginning, is now,
and will be forever. Amen.**

Phos Hilaron

O gracious Light, pure brightness of the ever-living Father in heaven, *
O Jesus Christ, holy and blessed!

Now as we have come to the setting of the sun, and our eyes behold the vesper light, *
We sing your praises, O God: Father, Son and Holy Spirit.

You are worthy at all times to be praised by happy voices, O Son of God, O Giver of life, *
And to be glorified through all the worlds.

December 28

Psalm   *(From Psalm 19)*

Truly He taught us to love one another;
His law is love and His Gospel is peace.

The heavens are telling the story of God; *
    And the firmament proclaims his handiwork.
Day to day pours forth speech, *
    And night to night declares knowledge.
Their voice goes out through all the earth, *
    And their words to the end of the world.
The law of the Lord is perfect, reviving the soul; *
    The decrees of the Lord are sure,
    making the wise simple;
The precepts of the Lord are right, rejoicing the heart;
    The commandment of the Lord is clear,
    enlightening the eyes;
Awe of the Lord is pure, enduring forever; *
    The ordinances of the Lord are true
    And righteous altogether.
More to be desired are they than gold,
even much fine gold; *
    Sweeter also than honey,
    and drippings of the honeycomb.
Let the words of my mouth and the meditation of my heart
be acceptable to you, *
    O Lord, my rock and my redeemer.

Glory to the Father, and to the Son,
and to the Holy Spirit. *
As it was in the beginning, is now,
and will be for ever. Amen.

Truly He taught us to love one another;
His law is love and His Gospel is peace.

II. The Lessons *(Be seated)*

Old Testament Lesson

A reading from the Book of Isaiah (65:17-25)

For I am about to create new heavens and a new earth; the former things shall not be remembered or come to mind. But be glad and rejoice forever in what I am creating; for I am about to create Jerusalem as a joy, and its people as a delight. I will rejoice in Jerusalem, and delight in my people; no more shall the sound of weeping be heard in it, or the cry of distress. No more shall there be in it an infant that lives but a few days, or an old person who does not live out a lifetime; for one who dies at a hundred years will be considered a youth, and one who falls short of a hundred will be considered unusual. They shall build houses and inhabit them; they shall plant vineyards and eat their fruit. Another shall not inhabit what they build, and another shall not eat what they plant; for like the days of a tree shall the days of my people be, and my chosen shall enjoy the work of their hands. They shall not labor in vain, or bear children for calamity; for they shall be offspring blessed by the Lord, as well as their descendants. Before they call, I will answer, while they are yet speaking I will hear. The wolf and the lamb shall feed together, the lion shall eat straw like the ox; but the serpent – its food shall be dust! They shall not hurt or destroy on all my holy mountain, says the Lord.

The word of the Lord.

Silence for reflection.

December 28

Canticle

O holy night, the stars are brightly shining;
It is the night of the dear Savior's birth!
Long lay the world in sin and error pining,
Till He appeared and the soul felt its worth.
A thrill of hope, the weary soul rejoices,
For yonder breaks a new and glorious morn.

Led by the light of faith serenely beaming,
With glowing hearts by His cradle we stand.
So led by light of a star sweetly gleaming,
Here came the wise men from Orient land.
The King of kings lay thus in lowly manger,
In all our trials born to be our friend!

Truly He taught us to love one another;
His law is love and His Gospel is peace.
Chains shall He break for the slave is our brother
And in His Name all oppression shall cease.
Sweet hymns of joy in grateful chorus raise we,
Let all within us praise His holy Name!

Fall on your knees, O hear the angel voices!
O night divine, O night when Christ was born!
O night, O holy night, O night divine!

December 28

Reading of the Gospel *(All stand)*

The Holy Gospel of Our Lord Jesus Christ according to Mark (10:13-16)

People were bringing little children to him in order that he might bless them; and the disciples spoke sternly to them. But when Jesus saw this, he was indignant and said to them, "Let the little children come to me; do not stop them; for it is such as these that the kingdom of God belongs. Truly I tell you, whoever does not receive the kingdom of God as a little child will never enter it." And he took them up in his arms, laid his hands on them, and blessed them.

The Gospel of the Lord.
Praise be to You, O Christ.

Silence for reflection, homily or reading. Be seated.

[How can we receive the kingdom of God as a little child?]

December 28

Magnificat

My soul proclaims the greatness of the Lord*
    My spirit rejoices in God my Savior.
You have looked with favor on your humble servant*
    And all generations will call me blessed.
You, O God, have done great things for me*
    And holy is your name.
You have mercy on those who love you*
    From generation to generation.
You have shown the strength of your arm*
    And have scattered the proud in their conceit.
You have cast down the mighty from their thrones*
    And have lifted up the lowly,
You have filled the hungry with good things*
    And the rich you have sent away empty.
You have come to the help of your people*
    For you remembered your promise of mercy.
The promise you made to our forbears*
    To Abraham and his children forever.

Lord, O Gracious Light!
Christ, O Precious Night!
Lord, O Gracious Light!

Hymn   (O Holy Night)

December 28

III. The Prayers

The Lord be with you.
And also with you.

The Lord's Prayer *(Stand facing altar)*

Our Father in heaven, hallowed be your name,
    Your kingdom come, your will be done,
    On earth as it is in heaven.
Give us today our daily bread.
Forgive us, as we forgive others.
Save us from the time of trial and deliver us from evil.
For the kingdom, the power, and the glory are yours
    Now and forever. Amen

Collect

Almighty God, heavenly Father, you have blessed us with the joy and care of children: Give us calm strength and patient wisdom as we bring them up, that we may teach them to love whatever is just and true and good, following the example of our Savior Jesus Christ, who lives and reigns with you, in the unity of the Holy Spirit, one God, for ever and ever. **Amen.**

Additional Prayers may be added here.

May the Lord bless us, keep us from evil, and lead us to eternal life. **Amen.**

Let us bless the Lord. **Thanks be to God.**

December 29
Thomas Becket

Born in London in 1118 of a wealthy Norman family and educated in England and in France. He became an administrator for Theobald, Archbishop of Canterbury. Later he was sent to study law in Italy and France and, after being ordained deacon, he was appointed Archdeacon of Canterbury. King Henry II caught notice of him and appointed him Chancellor of England. He and the king became good friends, and eventually King Henry secured Thomas' election as Archbishop of Canterbury in 1162. Eventually Thomas chose to defend the interests of the Church against those of his king. The struggle between the two became so bitter that Thomas sought exile at an abbey in France. He returned to England six years later following a fragile reconciliation with the king. Thomas was assassinated soon thereafter in the cathedral, allegedly on prompting by the king.

December 29

MORNING PRAYER

I. Invitatory

The officiant opens with this sentence: (All stand)

Jesus Christ is born! *
Glory to God in the highest!

Come Emmanuel!
God with us!

O Lord, Open our lips. *
And our mouth shall proclaim Your praise.

Glory to the Father, and to the Son,
and to the Holy Spirit. *
**As it was in the beginning, is now,
and will be for ever. Amen.**

Psalm

Rejoice! Rejoice! Emmanuel
Shall come to thee, O Israel.

Psalm 126

When the Lord restored the fortunes of Zion, *
    We were like those who dream.
Then our mouth was filled with laughter, *
    And our tongue with shouts of joy;
Then it was said among the nations, *
    "The Lord has done great things for them." *
The Lord has done great things for us, *
    And we rejoiced.
Restore our fortunes, O Lord, *
    Like the watercourses in the Negeb.
May those who sow in tears *
    Reap with shouts of joy.
Those who go out weeping, *
    Bearing the seed for sowing,
Shall come home with shouts of joy, *
    Carrying their sheaves.

Glory to the Father, and to the Son,
and to the Holy Spirit. *
As it was in the beginning, is now,
and will be for ever. Amen.

Rejoice! Rejoice! Emmanuel
Shall come to thee, O Israel.

II. The Lessons *(Be seated)*

Old Testament Lesson

A reading from the book of Isaiah (7:10-14)

Again the Lord spoke to Ahaz, saying, "Ask a sign of the Lord your God; let it be deep as Sheol or high as heaven." But Ahaz said, "I will not ask, and I will not put the Lord to the test." Then Isaiah said: "Hear then, O house of David! Is it too little for you to weary mortals, that you weary God also? Therefore the Lord himself will give you a sign. Look, the young woman is with child and shall bear a son, and shall name him Immanuel."

The word of the Lord.

Silence for reflection.

December 29

Canticle

O Come, O come, Emmanuel,
And ransom captive Israel,
That mourns in lonely exile here
Until the Son of God appear.

O come, Thou Rod of Jesse, free
Thine own from Satan's tyranny;
From depths of hell Thy people save,
And give them victory o'er the grave.

O come, Thou Day-Spring, come and cheer
Our spirits by Thine advent here;
Disperse the gloomy clouds of night
And death's dark shadows put to flight!

O come, Thou Key of David, come,
And open wide our heavenly home;
Make safe the way that leads on high,
And close the path to misery.

O come, O come, Thou Lord of Might,
Who to Thy tribes on Sinai's height
In ancient times didst give the law
In cloud, and majesty, and awe.
Rejoice! Rejoice! Emmanuel
Shall come to thee, O Israel.

December 29

Reading of the Gospel *(All stand)*

The Holy Gospel of Our Lord Jesus Christ according to Luke (2:1-7)

In those days a decree went out from Emperor Augustus that all the world should be registered. This was the first registration and was taken while Quirinius was governor of Syria. All the people went to their own towns to be registered. Joseph also went from the town of Nazareth in Galilee to Judea, to the city of David called Bethlehem, because he descended from the house and family of David. He went to be registered with Mary, to whom he was engaged and who was expecting a child. While they were there, the time came for her to deliver her child. And she gave birth to her firstborn son and wrapped him in bands of cloth, and laid him in a manger, because there was no place for them in the inn.

The Gospel of the Lord.
Praise be to You, O Christ.

Silence for reflection, homily or reading. Be seated.

[The ropes of your cincture may be pulled by God, leading you to places and situations you may not have planned on, much like what happened to Thomas Becket, Mary and Joseph. Are you willing to let this happen?]

December 29

Benedictus

Blessed are you O Lord our God*
> You have come to your people and set them free.

You have raised up for us a mighty Savior*
> Born of the house of your servant David.

Through your holy prophets you promised of old*
> That you would save us from our enemies,
> From the hands of all who hate us.

You promised to show mercy to our forbears*
> And to remember your holy covenant.

This was the oath you swore to our father Abraham*
> To set us free from the hands of our enemies,

Free to worship you without fear*
> Holy and righteous in your sight all the days of our life.

And you, child, shall be called the prophet of the Most High*
> For you will go before the Lord to prepare the way,

To give God's people knowledge of salvation*
> Through the forgiveness of their sins.

In the tender compassion of our God*
> The dawn from on high shall break upon us.

To shine on those who dwell in darkness and the shadow of death*
> And to guide our feet into the way of peace.

Glory to the Father, and to the Son,
and to the Holy Spirit. *
As it was in the beginning, is now,
and will be for ever. Amen.

Rejoice! Rejoice! Emmanuel
Shall come to thee, O Israel.

Hymn (O Come, O Come Emmanuel)

December 29

III. The Prayers

The Lord be with you all.
And also with you.

The Lord's Prayer *(Stand facing altar)*

Our Father in heaven, hallowed be your name,
    Your kingdom come, your will be done,
    On earth as it is in heaven.
Give us today our daily bread.
Forgive us, as we forgive others.
Save us from the time of trial and deliver us from evil.
For the kingdom, the power, and the glory are yours
    Now and forever. Amen

Collect

O God, our strength and our salvation, you called your servant Thomas Becket to be a shepherd of your people and a defender of your Church: Keep your household from all evil and raise up among us faithful pastors and leaders who are wise in the ways of the Gospel: through Jesus Christ the shepherd of our souls who lives and reigns with you and the Holy Spirit, one God, forever and ever. **Amen.**

Additional Prayers may be added here.

The grace of Our Lord Jesus Christ, and the love of God, and the companionship of the Holy Spirit, be in us and those absent from us. **Amen.**

Let us bless the Lord. **Thanks be to God.**

December 29

EVENING PRAYER

I. Invitatory

The officiant opens with this sentence: (All stand)

O God, make speed to save us.
O Lord, make haste to help us.

Glory to the Father, and to the Son,
and to the Holy Spirit. *
**As it was in the beginning, is now,
and will be for ever. Amen.**

Phos Hilaron

O gracious Light, pure brightness of the ever-living Father in heaven, *
O Jesus Christ, holy and blessed!

Now as we have come to the setting of the sun, and our eyes behold the vesper light, *
We sing your praises, O God: Father, Son and Holy Spirit.

You are worthy at all times to be praised by happy voices, O Son of God, O Giver of life, *
And to be glorified through all the worlds.

December 29

Psalm

Joy, joy for Christ is born,
The Babe, the Son of Mary.

Psalm 124

If it had not been the Lord who was defending us – *
    Let Israel now say,
If it had not been the Lord who was defending us, *
    When our enemies attacked us,
Then they would have swallowed us up alive, *
    When their anger was kindled against us;
Then the flood would have swept us away, *
    The torrent would have gone over us;
Then over us would have gone the raging waters. *
    Blessed be the Lord, who has not given us
    as prey to their teeth.
We have escaped like a bird from the snare of the fowlers; *
    The snare is broken, and we have escaped.
Our help is in the Name of the Lord, *
    Who made heaven and earth.

Glory to the Father, and to the Son,
and to the Holy Spirit. *
As it was in the beginning, is now,
and will be for ever. Amen.

Joy, joy for Christ is born,
The Babe, the Son of Mary.

December 29

II. The Lessons *(Be seated)*

Old Testament Lesson

A reading from the Book of Isaiah (52:7-10)

How beautiful upon the mountains are the feet of the messenger who announces peace, who brings good news, who announces salvation, who says to Zion, "Your God reigns." Listen! Your sentinels lift up their voices, together they sing for joy; for in plain sight they see the return of the Lord to Zion. Break forth together in singing, you ruins of Jerusalem; for the Lord has comforted his people, he has redeemed Jerusalem. The Lord has bared his holy arm before the eyes of all the nations; and all the ends of the earth shall see the salvation of our God.

The Word of the Lord.

Silence for reflection.

December 29

Canticle

What child is this who, laid to rest
On Mary's lap is sleeping?
Whom Angels greet with anthems sweet,
While shepherds watch are keeping?

This, this is Christ the King,
Whom shepherds guard and Angels sing;
Haste, haste, to bring Him laud,
The Babe, the Son of Mary.

Why lies He in such mean estate,
Where ox and ass are feeding?
Good Christians, fear, for sinners here
The silent Word is pleading.

Nails, spear shall pierce Him through,
The cross be borne for me, for you.
Hail, hail the Word made flesh,
The Babe, the Son of Mary.

So bring Him incense, gold and myrrh,
Come peasant, king to own Him;
The King of kings salvation brings,
Let loving hearts enthrone Him.

Raise, raise a song on high,
The virgin sings her lullaby.
Joy, joy for Christ is born,
The Babe, the Son of Mary.

December 29

Reading of the Gospel *(All stand)*

The Holy Gospel of Our Lord Jesus Christ according to John (7:37-42)

While Jesus was standing there, he said, "Let anyone who is thirsty come to me, and let the one who believes in me drink. As the scripture has said, 'Out of the believer's heart shall flow rivers of living water.'" When they heard these words, some in the crowd said, "This is really the prophet." Others said, "This is the Messiah." But some asked, "Surely the Messiah does not come from Galilee, does he? Has not the scripture said that the Messiah is descended from David and comes from Bethlehem, the village where David lived?"

The Gospel of the Lord.
Praise be to You, O Christ.

Silence for reflection, homily or reading. Be seated.

[Do you know how much God really loves you?]

December 29

Magnificat

My soul proclaims the greatness of the Lord*

    My spirit rejoices in God my Savior.

You have looked with favor on your humble servant*

    And all generations will call me blessed.

You, O God, have done great things for me*

    And holy is your name.

You have mercy on those who love you*

    From generation to generation.

You have shown the strength of your arm*

    And have scattered the proud in their conceit.

You have cast down the mighty from their thrones*

    And have lifted up the lowly,

You have filled the hungry with good things*

    And the rich you have sent away empty.

You have come to the help of your people*

    For you remembered your promise of mercy.

The promise you made to our forbears*

    To Abraham and his children forever.

Hymn (What Child is This?)

III. The Prayers

The Lord be with you.
And also with you.

The Lord's Prayer *(Stand facing altar)*

Our Father in heaven, hallowed be your name,
    Your kingdom come, your will be done,
    On earth as it is in heaven.
Give us today our daily bread.
Forgive us, as we forgive others.
Save us from the time of trial and deliver us from evil.
For the kingdom, the power, and the glory are yours
    Now and forever. Amen

Collect

O heavenly Father, who has filled the world with beauty; open our eyes to behold your gracious handiwork, rejoicing in your whole creation, that we may share its bounty as one family; through Jesus Christ the shepherd of our souls who lives and reigns with you and the Holy Spirit, one God, forever and ever. **Amen.**

Additional Prayers may be added here.

May the Lord bless us, keep us from evil, and lead us to eternal life. **Amen.**

Let us bless the Lord. **Thanks be to God.**

December 30
Frances Joseph-Gaudet

Frances as born in a log cabin in Holmesville, Mississippi, in 1861, of African American and Native American descent. While still a young woman, she dedicated her life to prison reform. In 1894 she began holding prayer meetings for prisoners, assisting them in writing letters, delivering messages, and getting them clothing. She later worked to rehabilitate young people arrested for minor offenses, becoming the first woman to support young offenders in Louisiana. Her efforts helped to found the Juvenile Court.

Deeply committed to the provision of good education, she eventually purchased a farm and founded the Gaudet Normal and Industrial School. In 1921 she donated the institution to the Episcopal Church. The Gaudet Episcopal Home opened in 1954. She died on December 30, 1934.

December 30

MORNING PRAYER

I. Invitatory

The officiant opens with this sentence: (All stand)

Jesus Christ is born! *
Glory to God in the highest!

Come Emmanuel!
God with us!

O Lord, Open our lips. *
And our mouth shall proclaim Your praise.

Glory to the Father, and to the Son,
and to the Holy Spirit. *
**As it was in the beginning, is now,
and will be for ever. Amen.**

Psalm

Go, tell it on the mountain
That Jesus Christ is born.

Psalm 24

The earth is the Lord's and all that is in it, *
    the world, and those who live in it;

December 30

For he has founded it on the seas, *
    and established it on the rivers.
Who shall ascend the hill of the Lord? *
    And who shall stand in his holy place?
Those who have clean hands and pure hearts, *
    who do not lift up their souls to what is false,
    and do not swear deceitfully.
They will receive blessing from the Lord, *
    and vindication from the God of their salvation.
Such are the people who seek him, *
    who seek the face of the God of Jacob.
Lift up your heads, O gates! *
    and be lifted up, O ancient doors!
That the King of glory may come in. *
    Who is the King of glory?
The Lord, strong and mighty, *
    the Lord, mighty in battle.
Lift up your heads, O gates! *
    and be lifted up, O ancient doors!
That the King of glory may come in. *
    Who is the King of glory?
The Lord of hosts, *
    he is the King of glory.

Glory to the Father, and to the Son,
and to the Holy Spirit. *
As it was in the beginning, is now,
and will be for ever. Amen.

Go, tell it on the mountain
That Jesus Christ is born.

II. The Lessons *(Be seated)*

Old Testament Lesson

A reading from the book of Isaiah (9:6-7)

For a child has been born for us, a son given to us; authority rests upon his shoulders; and he is named Wonderful Counselor, Mighty God, Everlasting Father, Prince of Peace. His authority shall grow continually, and there shall be endless peace for the throne of David and his kingdom. He will establish and uphold it with justice and with righteousness from this time onward and forever more. The zeal of the Lord of hosts will do this.

The word of the Lord.

Silence for reflection.

Canticle

While shepherds kept their watching
Over silent flocks by night,
Behold throughout the heavens
There shone a holy light

The shepherds feared and trembled
When lo, above the earth
Rang out the angel chorus
That hailed our Savior's birth;

Down in a lowly manger
The humble Christ was born;
And God sent out salvation
That blessed Christmas morn.

When I was a seeker
I sought both night and day
I sought the Lord to help me
And He showed me the way.

He made me a watchman
Upon the city wall
And if I am a Christian
I am the least of all.

Go, tell it on the mountain
Over the hills and everywhere
Go, tell it on the mountain
That Jesus Christ is born.

New Testament Lesson

A reading from the Book of Romans (15:7-13)

Welcome one another, therefore, just as Christ has welcomed you, for the glory of God. For I tell you that Christ has become a servant of the Jews on behalf of the truth of God in order that he might confirm the promises given to the patriarchs, and in order that the Gentiles might glorify God in his mercy. As it is written, "Therefore I will speak of you among the Gentiles, and sing praises to your name"; and again he says, "Rejoice, O Gentiles, with his people"; and again, "Praise the Lord, all you Gentiles, and let all people praise him"; and again Isaiah says, "The root of Jesse shall come, the one who rises to rule the Gentiles; in him the Gentile shall hope."

The word of the Lord.

Silence for reflection, homily or reading

[Isaiah used several names to describe the Lord. What names would you use to describe him in your life?]

December 30

Benedictus

Blessed are you O Lord our God*
You have come to your people and set them free.
You have raised up for us a mighty Savior*
Born of the house of your servant David.
Through your holy prophets you promised of old*
That you would save us from our enemies,
From the hands of all who hate us.
You promised to show mercy to our forbears*
And to remember your holy covenant.
This was the oath you swore to our father Abraham*
To set us free from the hands of our enemies,
Free to worship you without fear*
Holy and righteous in your sight all the days of our life.
And you, child, shall be called the prophet of the Most High*
For you will go before the Lord to prepare the way,
To give God's people knowledge of salvation*
Through the forgiveness of their sins.
In the tender compassion of our God*
The dawn from on high shall break upon us.
To shine on those who dwell in darkness and the shadow of death*
And to guide our feet into the way of peace.

Glory to the Father, and to the Son,
and to the Holy Spirit. *
As it was in the beginning, is now,
and will be for ever. Amen.

Hymn   (Go, Tell it on the Mountain)

December 30

III. The Prayers

The Lord be with you all.
And also with you.

The Lord's Prayer   *(Stand facing altar)*

Our Father in heaven, hallowed be your name,
    Your kingdom come, your will be done,
    On earth as it is in heaven.
Give us today our daily bread.
Forgive us, as we forgive others.
Save us from the time of trial and deliver us from evil.
For the kingdom, the power, and the glory are yours
    Now and forever. Amen

Collect

Merciful God, who raised up your servant Frances Joseph-Gaudet to work for prison reform and the education of her people: Grant that we, encouraged by the example of her life, may work for those who are denied the fullness of life for any reason: through Jesus Christ, who lives and reigns with you and the Holy Spirit, one God, for ever and ever. **Amen.**

Additional Prayers may be added here.

The grace of Our Lord Jesus Christ, and the love of God, and the companionship of the Holy Spirit, be in us and those absent from us. **Amen.**

Let us bless the Lord. **Thanks be to God.**

December 30

EVENING PRAYER

I. Invitatory

The officiant opens with this sentence: (All stand)

Glory to God in the highest heaven, *
and on earth peace among the people.

O God, make speed to save us.
O Lord, make haste to help us.

Glory to the Father, and to the Son,
and to the Holy Spirit. *
As it was in the beginning, is now,
and will be for ever. Amen.

Phos Hilaron

O gracious Light, pure brightness of the ever-living Father in heaven, *
O Jesus Christ, holy and blessed!

Now as we have come to the setting of the sun, and our eyes behold the vesper light, *
We sing your praises, O God: Father, Son and Holy Spirit.

You are worthy at all times to be praised by happy voices, O Son of God, O Giver of life, *
And to be glorified through all the worlds.

Psalm *(Be seated)*

All glory be to God on high, *
And on the earth be peace.

Psalm 23

The Lord is my shepherd, *
    I shall not be in need.
He makes me lie down in green pastures; *
    he leads me beside still waters;
and restores my soul; *
    He leads me along right paths
    for his name's sake. *
Even though I walk through the darkest valley, *
    I fear no evil, for you are with me.
Your rod and your staff - *
    They comfort me.
You prepare a table before me, *
    in the presence of my enemies;
You anoint my head with oil; *
    my cup overflows.
Surely goodness and mercy shall follow me, *
    all the days of my life,
And I shall dwell in the house of the Lord *
    my whole life long.

Glory to the Father, and to the Son,
and to the Holy Spirit. *
**As it was in the beginning, is now,
and will be for ever. Amen.**

All glory be to God on high, *
And on the earth be peace.

II. The Lessons

First Reading of the Gospel *(All stand)*

The Holy Gospel of Our Lord Jesus Christ according to Luke (2:8-14)

In that region there were shepherds living in the fields, keeping watch over their flock by night. Then an angel of the Lord stood before them, and the glory of the Lord shone around them, and they were terrified. But the angel said to them, "Do not be afraid; for see -- I am bringing you good news of great joy for all the people: to you is born this day in the city of David a Savior, who is the Messiah, the Lord. This will be a sign for you: you will find a child wrapped in bands of cloth and lying in a manger." And suddenly there was with the angel a multitude of the heavenly host, praising God and saying, "Glory to God in the highest heaven, and on earth peace among the people."

The Gospel of the Lord.
Praise be to You, O Christ.

Silence for reflection, homily or reading. Be seated.

December 30

Canticle

While Shepherds watch their flocks by night
All seated on the ground
The angel of the Lord came down
And glory shone around

"Fear not," said he for mighty dread
had seized their troubled mind
"Glad tidings of great joy I bring
To you and all man-kind.

"To you in David's town this day
Is born of David's line
The Savior who is Christ the Lord
And this shall me the sign

"The heavenly babe you there shall find
To human view displayed
All meanly wrapped in swathing bands
And in a manger laid."

Those spoke the seraph and forth-with
Appeared a shining throng
Of angels praising God who thus
Addressed their joyful song

"All glory be to God on high
And on the earth be peace
Goodwill hence-forth from heaven to men
Begin and never cease."

Second Reading of the Gospel *(All stand)*

The Holy Gospel of Our Lord Jesus Christ according to Luke (2:15-20)

When the angels had left them and gone into heaven, the shepherds said to one another, "Let us go now to Bethlehem and see this thing that has taken place, which the Lord has made known to us." So they went with haste and found Mary and Joseph, and the child lying in the manger. When they saw this, they made known what had been told them about this child; and all who heard it were amazed at what the shepherds told them. But Mary treasured all these words and pondered them in her heart. The shepherds returned, glorifying and praising God for all they had heard and seen, as it had been told them.

The Gospel of the Lord.
Praise be to You, O Christ.

Silence for reflection, homily or reading. Be seated.

[Why is the birth of the Messiah "good news and great joy" for you?]

December 30

Magnificat

My soul proclaims the greatness of the Lord*
    My spirit rejoices in God my Savior.
You have looked with favor on your humble servant*
    And all generations will call me blessed.
You, O God, have done great things for me*
    And holy is your name.
You have mercy on those who love you*
    From generation to generation.
You have shown the strength of your arm*
    And have scattered the proud in their conceit.
You have cast down the mighty from their thrones*
    And have lifted up the lowly,
You have filled the hungry with good things*
    And the rich you have sent away empty.
You have come to the help of your people*
    For you remembered your promise of mercy.
The promise you made to our forbears*
To Abraham and his children forever.

Lord, O Gracious Light!
Christ, O Perfect Love!
Lord, O Gracious Light!

Hymn (While Shepherds watch their flocks by night)

December 30

III. The Prayers

The Lord be with you.
And also with you.

The Lord's Prayer   *(Stand facing altar)*

Our Father in heaven, hallowed be your name,
    Your kingdom come, your will be done,
    On earth as it is in heaven.
Give us today our daily bread.
Forgive us, as we forgive others.
Save us from the time of trial and deliver us from evil.
For the kingdom, the power, and the glory are yours
    Now and forever. Amen

Collect

Almighty God, we entrust all who are dear to us to your never-failing care and love, for this life and the life to come, knowing that you are doing for them better things than we can even desire or pray for; through Jesus Christ, who lives and reigns with you and the Holy Spirit, one God, forever and ever. **Amen.**

Additional Prayers may be added here.

May the God of hope fill you with all joy and peace in believing, so that you may abound in hope by the power of the Holy Spirit.   **Amen.**

Let us bless the Lord.   **Thanks be to God.**

December 31

MORNING PRAYER

I. Invitatory

The officiant opens with this sentence: (All stand)

Alleluia! To us a child is born! *
Come let us adore him. Alleluia!

O Lord, Open our lips. *
And our mouth shall proclaim Your praise.

Glory to the Father, and to the Son,
and to the Holy Spirit. *
**As it was in the beginning, is now,
and will be for ever. Amen.**

Psalm

Let us all with one accord *
Sing praises to our heavenly Lord.

Psalm 46

God is our refuge and strength, *
    a very present help in trouble.

December 31

Therefore we will not fear, *
>though the earth should change,

Though the mountains shake *
>in the heart of the sea;

though its waters roar and foam, *
>though the mountains tremble with its tumult.

There is a river whose streams make glad the city of God, *
>the holy habitation of the Most High.

God is in the midst of the city;
it shall not be moved; *
>God will help it when the morning dawns.

The nations are in an uproar, the kingdoms totter; *
>he utters his voice, the earth melts.

The Lord of hosts is with us; *
>the God of Jacob is our refuge.

Come, behold the works of the Lord; *
>see what changes he has brought on the earth.

He stops wars throughout the earth; *
>he breaks the bow, and shatters the spear,
>and he burns the shields with fire.

"Be still and know that I am God! *
>I am exalted among the nations,
>I am exalted in the earth."

The Lord of hosts is with us; *
>the God of Jacob is our refuge.

Glory to the Father, and to the Son,
and to the Holy Spirit. *
**As it was in the beginning, is now,
and will be for ever. Amen.**

Let us all with one accord *
Sing praises to our heavenly Lord.

II. The Lessons *(Be seated)*

Old Testament Lesson

A reading from the book of Jeremiah (23:5-6)

The days are surely coming, says the Lord, when I will raise up for David a righteous Branch, and he shall reign as king and deal wisely, and shall execute justice and righteousness in the land. In his days Judah will be saved and Israel will live in safety. And this is the name by which he will be called: "The Lord is our Righteousness."

The word of the Lord.

Silence for reflection.

Canticle

The first Noel the Angel did say
Was to three poor Shepherds in fields as they lay.
In fields where they lay keeping their sheep,
In a cold winter's night that was so deep.

December 31

They looked up and saw a star
Shining in the East, beyond them far,
And to the earth it gave great light,
And so it continued, both day and night.

And by the light of that same star
Three wise men came from country far,
To seek for a King was their intent,
And to follow the star wherever it went.

This star drew nigh to the North West;
Over Bethlehem it took its rest.
And there it did both stop and stay,
Right over the place where Jesus lay.

Then let us all with one accord
Sing praises to our heavenly Lord;
That hath made heaven and earth of naught,
And with his blood mankind hath bought.

If we in our time shall do well
We shall be free from death and Hell
For God hath prepared for us all
A resting place in general.
Noel, noel, noel, noel,
Born is the King of Israel.

December 31

New Testament Lesson

A reading from the Book of 1 John (5:1-8)

Everyone who believes that Jesus is the Christ has been born of God, and everyone who loves the parent loves the child. By this we know that we love the children of God, when we love God and obey his commandments. And his commandments are not burdensome, for whatever is born of God conquers the world. And this is the victory that conquers the world, our faith. Who is it that conquers the world but the one who believes that Jesus is the Son of God? This is the one who came by water and blood, Jesus Christ, not with the water only but with the water and the blood. And the Spirit is the one that testifies, for the Spirit is the truth. There are three that testify: the Spirit and the water and the blood, and these three agree.

The word of the Lord.

Silence for reflection, homily or reading

[The body and blood we receive at the Holy Eucharist IS the real body and blood of Christ - but remember that he is no longer in the flesh, so this real body and blood is now of a spiritual nature, coming to us through the common earthly elements of bread and wine. It is meant to bind our souls with the Holy Spirit, make our flesh Christ's new flesh, thereby binding the spiritual and the physical realms. We are renewed with the faith that helps us add goodness to the world around us. How will you use this power in the coming year?]

Benedictus

Blessed are you O Lord our God*
You have come to your people and set them free.
You have raised up for us a mighty Savior*
Born of the house of your servant David.
Through your holy prophets you promised of old*
That you would save us from our enemies,
From the hands of all who hate us.
You promised to show mercy to our forbears*
And to remember your holy covenant.
This was the oath you swore to our father Abraham*
To set us free from the hands of our enemies,
Free to worship you without fear*
Holy and righteous in your sight all the days of our life.
And you, child, shall be called the prophet of the Most High*
For you will go before the Lord to prepare the way,
To give God's people knowledge of salvation*
Through the forgiveness of their sins.
In the tender compassion of our God*
The dawn from on high shall break upon us.
To shine on those who dwell in darkness and the shadow of death*
And to guide our feet into the way of peace.

Glory to the Father, and to the Son,
and to the Holy Spirit. *
**As it was in the beginning, is now,
and will be for ever. Amen.**

Hymn   (The First Noel)

III. The Prayers

The Lord be with you all.
And also with you.

The Lord's Prayer *(Stand facing altar)*

Our Father in heaven, hallowed be your name,
    Your kingdom come, your will be done,
    On earth as it is in heaven.
Give us today our daily bread.
Forgive us, as we forgive others.
Save us from the time of trial and deliver us from evil.
For the kingdom, the power, and the glory are yours
    Now and forever. Amen

Collect

O Lord Jesus Christ, who in a wonderful Sacrament has left unto us a memorial of your passion: Grant us so to venerate these sacred mysteries of your Body and Blood, that we may ever perceive within ourselves the fruit of Your redemption; who lives and reigns with the Father and the Holy Spirit, one God, for ever and ever. **Amen.**

Additional Prayers may be added here.

The grace of Our Lord Jesus Christ, and the love of God, and the companionship of the Holy Spirit, be in us and those absent from us. **Amen.**

Let us bless the Lord. **Thanks be to God.**

December 31

EVENING PRAYER

I. Invitatory

The officiant opens with this sentence: (All stand)

O God, make speed to save us.
O Lord, make haste to help us.

Glory to the Father, and to the Son,
and to the Holy Spirit. *
As it was in the beginning, is now,
and will be forever. Amen.

Phos Hilaron

O gracious Light, pure brightness of the ever-living Father in heaven, *
O Jesus Christ, holy and blessed!

Now as we have come to the setting of the sun, and our eyes behold the vesper light, *
We sing your praises, O God: Father, Son and Holy Spirit.

You are worthy at all times to be praised by happy voices, O Son of God, O Giver of life, *
And to be glorified through all the worlds.

Psalm

In the dark streets of life, *
shines the everlasting Light.

Psalm 93

The Lord is King, *
    he is robed in majesty;
The Lord is robed, *
    he is girded with strength.
He has established the world; *
    it shall never be moved.
Your throne is established from old; *
    You are from everlasting.
The floods have lifted up, O Lord, *
    the floods have lifted up their voice;
The floods lift up their roaring, *
    more majestic than the thunders of mighty waters,
More majestic than the waves of the sea, *
    majestic on high is the Lord!
Your decrees are very sure; *
    holiness befits your house,
O Lord, forevermore.

Glory to the Father, and to the Son,
and to the Holy Spirit. *
As it was in the beginning, is now,
and will be for ever. Amen.

In the dark streets of life, *
shines the everlasting Light.

II. The Lessons *(Be seated)*

Old Testament Lesson

A reading from the Book of Genesis (1:1-5)

In the beginning God created the heavens and the earth, the earth had been a formless void and darkness covered the face of the deep, while the Spirit of God swept over the face of the waters. Then God said, "Let there be light"; and there was light. And God saw that the light was good; and God separated the light from the darkness. God called the light day, and the darkness he called night. And there was evening and there was morning, the first day.

The Word of the Lord.

Silence for reflection.

Canticle

O little town of Bethlehem,
How still we see thee lie!
Above thy deep and dreamless sleep
The silent stars go by.
Yet in thy dark streets shines
The everlasting Light;
The hopes and fears of all the years
Are met in thee to-night.

December 31

O morning stars, together
Proclaim the holy birth!
And praises sing to God the King,
And peace to men on earth.
For Christ is born of Mary
And gathered all above,
While mortals sleep the angels keep
Their watch of wondering love.

How silently, how silently,
The wondrous gift is given;
So God imparts to human hearts
The blessings of His Heaven.
No ear may hear His coming,
But in this world of sin,
Where meek souls will receive Him still,
The dear Christ enters in.

Where children pure and happy
Pray to the blessed Child,
Where misery cries out to Thee,
Son of the Mother mild;
Where Charity stands watching
And Faith holds wide the door,
The dark night wakes, the glory breaks,
And Christmas comes once more.

O Holy Child of Bethlehem,
Descend to us, we pray!
Cast out our sin and enter in,
Be born in us to-day.
We hear the Christmas angels,
The great glad tidings tell;
O come to us, abide with us,
Our Lord Emmanuel!

December 31

Reading of the Gospel *(All stand)*

The Holy Gospel of Our Lord Jesus Christ according to John (1:1-5)

In the beginning was the Word, and the Word was with God, and the Word was God. He was in the beginning with God. All things came into being through him, and without him not one thing came into being. What has come into being in him was life, and the life was the light of all people. The light shines in the darkness, and the darkness did not overcome it.

The Gospel of the Lord.
Praise be to You, O Christ.

Silence for reflection, homily or reading. Be seated.

[What are some of the ways you can let the Light of God shine in your heart, transforming you moment by moment?]

Magnificat

My soul proclaims the greatness of the Lord*
    My spirit rejoices in God my Savior.
You have looked with favor on your humble servant*
    And all generations will call me blessed.
You, O God, have done great things for me*
    And holy is your name.
You have mercy on those who love you*
    From generation to generation.
You have shown the strength of your arm*
    And have scattered the proud in their conceit.
You have cast down the mighty from their thrones*
    And have lifted up the lowly,
You have filled the hungry with good things*
    And the rich you have sent away empty.
You have come to the help of your people*
    For you remembered your promise of mercy.
The promise you made to our forbears*
To Abraham and his children forever.

Lord, O Gracious Light!
Christ, O Perfect Love!
Lord, O Gracious Light!

Hymn   (O Little Town of Bethlehem)

December 31

III. The Prayers

The Lord be with you.
And also with you.

The Lord's Prayer   *(Stand facing altar)*

Our Father in heaven, hallowed be your name,
>   Your kingdom come, your will be done,
>   On earth as it is in heaven.
Give us today our daily bread.
Forgive us, as we forgive others.
Save us from the time of trial and deliver us from evil.
For the kingdom, the power, and the glory are yours
>   Now and forever. Amen

Collect

Almighty and everliving God, let your fatherly hand ever be over these your children; let your Holy Spirit ever be their Light; and so lead them in the knowledge and love of your Word, that they may serve you in their own unique way in this life and the next; through Jesus Christ, who lives and reigns with you and the Holy Spirit, one God now and forever more. **Amen.**

Additional Prayers may be added here.

May the God of hope fill you with all joy and peace in believing, so that you may abound in hope by the power of the Holy Spirit. **Amen.**

Let us bless the Lord. **Thanks be to God.**

January 1
The Holy Name
of Our Lord

The designation of this day as the Feast of the Holy Name is new to the 1979 Book of Common Prayer. January 1st is the eighth day after Christmas Day, and the Gospel according to Luke records the circumcision and the naming. It had long been the custom to make this a festive occasion, when family and friends came together to witness the naming of the child. In the Roman tradition, January 1st was observed as the octave day of Christmas, and it was devoted to the Virgin Mother.

The name was given to Jesus, as the angel explained to Joseph, because he would "save his people from their darkness, and bring them back into the Light." Then, as now, people longed to be freed from evils: political, social, and spiritual. The name Jesus calls to mind the true freedom which is ours through Jesus Christ.

January 1

MORNING PRAYER

I. Invitatory

The officiant opens with this sentence: (All stand)

Alleluia! To us a child is born! *
Come let us adore him. Alleluia!

O Lord, Open our lips. *
And our mouth shall proclaim Your praise.

Glory to the Father, and to the Son,
and to the Holy Spirit. *
As it was in the beginning, is now,
and will be for ever. Amen.

Psalm

Glad tidings to all,
Our King has been born!

Psalm 103

Bless the Lord, O my soul, and all that is within me, *
    Bless his holy name.
Bless the Lord, O my soul, *
    and do not forget all his benefits.
Who forgives all your iniquity, *
    who heals all your diseases,
Who redeems your life from the Pit, *
    who crowns you with steadfast love and mercy,
Who satisfies you with good as long as you live, *
    so that your youth is renewed like the eagle's.

January 1

The Lord works vindication, *
    and gives justice to the oppressed.
He made known his ways to Moses, *
    his acts to the people of Israel.
The Lord is merciful and gracious, *
    slow to anger and abounding
    in steadfast love.
He will not always accuse, *
    nor will he keep his anger forever.
He overlooks our waywardness, *
    and deals with us fairly.
For as the heavens are high above the earth, *
    so great is his steadfast love
    toward those who honestly seek him.
As far as the east is from the west, *
    so he removes the darkness from us.
As a father has compassion for his children, *
    so the Lord has compassion for his children.
For he knows how we were made; *
    he remembers that we are dust.
As for mortals, their days are like grass; *
    they flourish like a flower of the field;
For the wind passes over it, and it is gone, *
    and its place knows it no more.
But the steadfast love of the Lord *
    is from everlasting to everlasting.
His righteousness given to the children's children, *
    to those who remember to live his way.
The Lord has established his throne in the heavens, *
    and his kingdom rules over all.
Bless the Lord, O you his angels,
    you mighty ones who do his bidding.

Glory to the Father, and to the Son,
and to the Holy Spirit. *
**As it was in the beginning, is now,
and will be for ever. Amen.**

Glad tidings to all,
Our King has been born!

II. The Lessons *(Be seated)*

Old Testament Lesson

A reading from the book of Jeremiah (30:21-22)

Their prince shall be one of their own, their ruler shall come from their midst; I will bring him near, and he shall approach me, for who would otherwise dare to approach me? says the Lord. And you shall be my people, and I will be your God.

The word of the Lord.

Silence for reflection.

Canticle

A child this day is born
A child of high renown
Most worthy of a scepter and a crown

These tidings shepherds heard
Whilst watching o'er their fold;
'Twas by an Angel unto them
That night revealed and told.

Then was there with the Angel
A host innumerable
Of heavenly bright soldiers,
All from the highest sent.

They praised the Lord our God,
And our celestial King;
All glory be in Paradise,
This heavenly host do sing.

All glory be to God,
That sits bright on high,
With praises and with triumph great,
And joyful melody.

Glad tidings to all men
Glad tidings sing we may
Because the king of kings
Was born on Christmas day

January 1

New Testament Lesson

A reading from the Book of Philippians (2:5-11)

Let the same mind be in you that was in Christ Jesus, who, even though he was in the form of God, did not regard this as something to be exploited; but he 'emptied himself,' humbled himself, taking the form of a servant, being born in human likeness. And being found in human form, he became obedient to the point of death - the death on a cross. Therefore God also highly exalted him and gave him the name that is above every name, so that at the name of Jesus every knee should bend, in heaven and on earth and under the earth, and every tongue should confess that Jesus Christ is Lord, to the glory of God the Father.

The word of the Lord.

Silence for reflection, homily or reading.

[By practicing non-judgmental self-awareness, we, too, can work to empty ourselves and become better servants of God. How can you better practice this during the coming year?]

Benedictus

Blessed are you O Lord our God*
You have come to your people and set them free.
You have raised up for us a mighty Savior*
Born of the house of your servant David.
Through your holy prophets you promised of old*
That you would save us from our enemies,
From the hands of all who hate us.
You promised to show mercy to our forbears*
And to remember your holy covenant.
This was the oath you swore to our father Abraham*
To set us free from the hands of our enemies,
Free to worship you without fear*
Holy and righteous in your sight all the days of our life.
And you, child, shall be called the prophet of the Most High*
For you will go before the Lord to prepare the way,
To give God's people knowledge of salvation*
Through the forgiveness of their sins.
In the tender compassion of our God*
The dawn from on high shall break upon us.
To shine on those who dwell in darkness and the shadow of death*
And to guide our feet into the way of peace.

Glory to the Father, and to the Son,
and to the Holy Spirit. *
As it was in the beginning, is now,
and will be for ever. Amen.

Hymn (A Child This Day is Born)

III. The Prayers

The Lord be with you all.
And also with you.

The Lord's Prayer *(Stand facing altar)*

Our Father in heaven, hallowed be your name,
    Your kingdom come, your will be done,
    On earth as it is in heaven.
Give us today our daily bread.
Forgive us, as we forgive others.
Save us from the time of trial and deliver us from evil.
For the kingdom, the power, and the glory are yours
    Now and forever. Amen

Collect

Eternal Father, you gave to your incarnate Son the holy name of Jesus to be the sign of our salvation: Plant in every heart, we pray, the love of him who is the Savior of the world, our Lord Jesus Christ; who lives and reigns with you and the Holy Spirit, one God, in glory everlasting. **Amen.**

Additional Prayers may be added here.

The grace of Our Lord Jesus Christ, and the love of God, and the companionship of the Holy Spirit, be in us and those absent from us. **Amen.**

Let us bless the Lord. **Thanks be to God.**

EVENING PRAYER

I. Invitatory

The officiant opens with this sentence: (All stand)

O God, make speed to save us.
O Lord, make haste to help us.

Glory to the Father, and to the Son,
and to the Holy Spirit. *
**As it was in the beginning, is now,
and will be for ever. Amen.**

Phos Hilaron

O gracious Light, pure brightness of the ever-living Father in heaven, *
O Jesus Christ, holy and blessed!

Now as we have come to the setting of the sun, and our eyes behold the vesper light, *
We sing your praises, O God: Father, Son and Holy Spirit.

You are worthy at all times to be praised by happy voices, O Son of God, O Giver of life, *
And to be glorified through all the worlds.

January 1

Psalm *Psalm 148 (1-13)*

Hail Mary, full of grace,
the Lord is with thee.

Praise the Lord! Praise him from the heavens; *
    Praise him from the heights!
Praise him, all his angels; *
    praise him, all his host!
Praise him, sun and moon; *
    praise him all you shining stars!
Praise him, you highest heavens, *
    and you waters above the heavens!
Let them praise the name of the Lord, *
    for he commanded and they created.
He established them forever and ever; *
    he set their bounds, which cannot be passed.
Praise the Lord from the earth, *
    you sea monsters and all deeps,
Fire and hail, snow and frost, *
    stormy wind fulfilling his command!
Mountains and all hills, *
    fruit trees and all cedars!
Wild animals and all cattle, *
    creeping things and flying birds!
Kings of the earth and all peoples, *
    princes and all rulers of the earth!
Men and women alike, *
    old and young together!
Let them praise the name of the Lord, *
    for his name is exalted.

Glory to the Father, and to the Son,
and to the Holy Spirit. *
As it was in the beginning, is now,
and will be for ever. Amen.

Hail Mary, full of grace,
the Lord is with thee.

II. The Lessons

First Reading of the Gospel *(All stand)*

The Holy Gospel of Our Lord Jesus Christ according to Luke (2:21-24)

After eight days had passed, it was time to circumcise the child; and he was called Jesus, the name given by the angel before he was conceived in the womb. When the time came for their purification according to the law of Moses, they brought him up to Jerusalem to present him to the Lord (as it was written in the law of the Lord, "Every firstborn male shall be designated as holy to the Lord"), and they offered a sacrifice according to what is stated in the law of the Lord, "a pair of turtledoves or two young pigeons."

The Gospel of the Lord.
Praise be to You, O Christ.

Silence for reflection.

Canticle

Hail Mary, full of grace, the Lord is with thee;
    blessed art thou amongst women,
    and blessed is the fruit of thy womb, Jesus.
Holy Mary, Mother of God,
    pray for us sinners now
    and at the hour of our death.

Second Reading of the Gospel

The Holy Gospel of Our Lord Jesus Christ according to Luke (2:25-33)

Now there was a man in Jerusalem whose name was Simeon; this man was righteous and devout, looking forward to the consolation of Israel, and the Holy Spirit rested on him. It had been revealed to him by the Holy Spirit that he would not see death before he had seen the Lord's Messiah. Guided by the Spirit, Simeon came into the temple; and when the parents brought in the child Jesus, to do for him what was customary under the law, Simeon took him into his arms and praised God, saying, "Master, now your servant may depart in peace according to your word; for my eyes have seen your salvation, which you have prepared in the presence of all peoples, a light for revelation to the Gentiles, and for the glory to your people Israel." And the child's father and mother were amazed at what was being said about him.

The Gospel of the Lord.
Praise be to You, O Christ.

January 1

Silence for reflection, homily or reading. Be seated.

[God knows you by name. What does your own name mean to you as you seek to know, love, and serve the Lord in your own unique way?]

Magnificat

My soul proclaims the greatness of the Lord*
    My spirit rejoices in God my Savior.
You have looked with favor on your humble servant*
    And all generations will call me blessed.
You, O God, have done great things for me*
    And holy is your name.
You have mercy on those who love you*
    From generation to generation.
You have shown the strength of your arm*
    And have scattered the proud in their conceit.
You have cast down the mighty from their thrones*
    And have lifted up the lowly,
You have filled the hungry with good things*
    And the rich you have sent away empty.
You have come to the help of your people*
    For you remembered your promise of mercy.
The promise you made to our forbears*
To Abraham and his children forever.

Lord, O Gracious Light!
Christ, O Perfect Love!
Lord, O Gracious Light!

Hymn (Ave Maria)

III. The Prayers

The Lord be with you.
And also with you.

The Lord's Prayer   *(Stand facing altar)*

Our Father in heaven, hallowed be your name,
> Your kingdom come, your will be done,
> On earth as it is in heaven.
Give us today our daily bread.
Forgive us, as we forgive others.
Save us from the time of trial and deliver us from evil.
For the kingdom, the power, and the glory are yours
> Now and forever. Amen

Collect

Almighty God, you have poured upon us the new light of your incarnate Word: Grant that this light, enkindled in our hearts, may shine forth in our lives; through Jesus Christ our Lord, who lives and reigns with you, in the unity of the Holy Spirit, one God, now and for ever. **Amen.**

Additional Prayers may be added here.

May the God of hope fill you with all joy and peace in believing, so that you may abound in hope by the power of the Holy Spirit. **Amen.**

Let us bless the Lord.   **Thanks be to God.**

January 2

MORNING PRAYER

I. Invitatory

The officiant opens with this sentence: (All stand)

Alleluia! To us a child is born! *
Come let us adore him. Alleluia!

O Lord, Open our lips. *
And our mouth shall proclaim Your praise.

Glory to the Father, and to the Son,
and to the Holy Spirit. *
**As it was in the beginning, is now,
and will be for ever. Amen.**

Psalm

Joy to the world, the Lord is come;
Let earth receive her King.

Psalm 47

Clap your hands, all you peoples; *
    shout to God with loud songs of joy.
For the Lord, the Most High, is awesome, *
    a great king over all the earth.
He subdued peoples under us, *
    and nations under our feet.
Chose our heritage for us, *
    the pride of Jacob whom he loves.
God has gone up with a shout, *
    the Lord with the sound of a trumpet.
Sing praises to God, sing praises; *
    sing praises to our King, sing praises.
For God is the king of all the earth; *
    sing praises with a psalm.
God is king over the nations; *
    God sits on his holy throne.
The princes of the peoples gather *
    as the people of the God of Abraham.
For the shields of the earth belong to God; *
    he is highly exalted.

Glory to the Father, and to the Son,
and to the Holy Spirit. *
As it was in the beginning, is now,
and will be for ever. Amen.

Joy to the world, the Lord is come;
Let earth receive her King.

January 2

II. The Lessons *(Be seated)*

Old Testament Lesson

A reading from the book of Isaiah (11:1-9)

    A shoot shall come out from the family Jesse, and a branch shall grow out of his roots. The spirit of the Lord shall rest on him, the spirit of wisdom and understanding, the spirit of counsel and might, the spirit of knowledge and an awe of the Lord. His delight shall be in the awesomeness of the Lord. He shall not judge by what his eyes see, or decide by what his ears hear; but with righteousness he shall judge the poor, and decide with equity for the meek of the earth; he shall strike the earth with the rod of his mouth, and with the breath of his lips he shall destroy the wicked.
    Righteousness shall be the belt around his waist, and faithfulness the belt around his loins. The wolf shall live with the lamb, the leopard shall lie down with the kid, the calf and the lion and the fatling together, and a little child shall lead them. The cow and the bear shall graze, their young shall lie down together; and the lion shall eat straw like the ox. The nursing child shall play over the hole of the asp, and the weaned child shall put its hand in the adder's den. They will not hurt or destroy on all my holy mountain; for the earth will be full of the knowledge of the Lord as waters cover the sea.

The word of the Lord.

Silence for reflection.

Canticle

Joy to the world, the Lord is come;
Let earth receive her King;
Let every heart prepare Him room,
And heaven, and heaven and nature sing.

Joy to the earth, the Savior reigns;
Let men their songs employ;
While fields and floods,
Rocks, hills and plains
Repeat, repeat the sounding joy.

No more let sins and sorrows grow,
Nor thorns infest the ground;
He comes to make His blessing flow
Far as, far as the curse is found.

He rules the world with truth and grace,
And makes the nations prove
The glories of His righteousness,
And wonders, wonders of His love.

New Testament Lesson

A reading from the Book of 1 John (2:12-14)

I am writing to you, little children, because you are forgiven on account of his name. I am writing to you, fathers, because you know him who is from the beginning. I am writing to you, young people, because you have conquered the evil one. I am writing to you, children, because you know the Father. I am writing to you, fathers, because you know him who is from the beginning. I am writing to you, young people, because you are strong and the word of God abides in you, and you have overcome the evil one.

The word of the Lord.

Silence for reflection, homily or reading.

[The birth of Christ signals a new world - a new way of thinking and being; a new way of living, and a new way of loving. How can you remain open to the changes God has in store for you this coming year?]

Benedictus

Blessed are you O Lord our God*
You have come to your people and set them free.
You have raised up for us a mighty Savior*
Born of the house of your servant David.
Through your holy prophets you promised of old*
That you would save us from our enemies,
From the hands of all who hate us.
You promised to show mercy to our forbears*
And to remember your holy covenant.
This was the oath you swore to our father Abraham*
To set us free from the hands of our enemies,
Free to worship you without fear*
Holy and righteous in your sight all the days of our life.
And you, child, shall be called the prophet of the Most High*
For you will go before the Lord to prepare the way,
To give God's people knowledge of salvation*
Through the forgiveness of their sins.
In the tender compassion of our God*
The dawn from on high shall break upon us.
To shine on those who dwell in darkness and the shadow of death*
And to guide our feet into the way of peace.

Glory to the Father, and to the Son,
and to the Holy Spirit. *
As it was in the beginning, is now,
and will be for ever. Amen.

Hymn   (Joy to the World)

III. The Prayers

The Lord be with you all.
And also with you.

The Lord's Prayer   *(Stand facing altar)*

Our Father in heaven, hallowed be your name,
    Your kingdom come, your will be done,
    On earth as it is in heaven.
Give us today our daily bread.
Forgive us, as we forgive others.
Save us from the time of trial and deliver us from evil.
For the kingdom, the power, and the glory are yours
    Now and forever. Amen

Collect

Almighty God, who has sent us the gift of Christ: help us to remain open to your presence in our lives, and be accepting of what changes you make in our thoughts, words and deeds; through Jesus Christ our Lord, who lives and reigns with you and the Holy Spirit, one God, now and forever. **Amen.**

Additional Prayers may be added here.

The grace of Our Lord Jesus Christ, and the love of God, and the companionship of the Holy Spirit, be in us and those absent from us.   **Amen.**

Let us bless the Lord.   **Thanks be to God.**

January 2

EVENING PRAYER

I. Invitatory

The officiant opens with this sentence: (All stand)

O God, make speed to save us.
O Lord, make haste to help us.

Glory to the Father, and to the Son,
and to the Holy Spirit. *
**As it was in the beginning, is now,
and will be for ever. Amen.**

Phos Hilaron

O gracious Light, pure brightness of the ever-living Father in heaven, *
O Jesus Christ, holy and blessed!

Now as we have come to the setting of the sun, and our eyes behold the vesper light, *
We sing your praises, O God: Father, Son and Holy Spirit.

You are worthy at all times to be praised by happy voices, O Son of God, O Giver of life, *
And to be glorified through all the worlds.

January 2

Psalm

Silent night, holy night!
All is calm, all is bright.

Psalm 33

Rejoice in the Lord, O you righteous. *
    Praise befits the upright.
Praise the Lord with the lyre; *
    make melody with the ten-string harp.
Sing to him a new song; *
    play skillfully on the strings with shouts.
For the word of the Lord is upright, *
    and all his work is done in faithfulness.
He loves righteousness and justice; *
    the earth is full of the steadfast love of the Lord.
By the word of the Lord the heavens were made, *
    and all their host by the breath of his mouth.
He gathered the waters of the sea as in a bottle; *
    he put the deeps in storehouses.
Let all the earth awe the Lord; *
    let all the peoples stand in awe of him.
For he spoke, and it came to be; *
    he commanded, and it stood firm.
The Lord makes the wisdom of the nations small; *
    He frustrates the plans of the peoples.
But the counsel of the Lord stands forever, *
    the thoughts of his heart to all generations.
Happy is the nation whose God is the Lord, *
    the people whom he has chosen as his heritage.

January 2

The Lord looks down from heaven; *
    he sees all humankind.
He who fashions the hearts of them all, *
    and observes their deeds.
A king is not saved by his great army; *
    a warrior is not delivered by his strength.
The war horse is a vain hope for victory, *
    and by its great might it cannot save.
Truly the Lord sees those who love him, *
    He delivers their soul from death.
Our soul waits for the Lord; *
    he is our help and shield.
Our heart is glad in him because we trust him.*
    Let your steadfast love be upon us, O Lord.

Glory to the Father, and to the Son,
and to the Holy Spirit. *
As it was in the beginning, is now,
and will be for ever. Amen.

Silent night, holy night!
All is calm, all is bright.

II. The Lessons

First Reading of the Gospel *(All stand.)*

The Holy Gospel of Our Lord Jesus Christ according to Luke (2:36-39)

There was also a prophet, Anna the daughter of Phanuel, of the tribe of Asher. She was of great age, having lived with her husband seven years after her marriage, then was a widow to the age of eighty-four. She never left the temple but worshipped there with fasting and prayer night and day. At that moment (when Jesus was brought to the temple eight days after his birth) she came, and began to praise God and to speak about the child to all who were looking for the redemption of Jerusalem. When they had finished everything required by the law of the Lord, they returned to Galilee, to their own town of Nazareth.

The Gospel of the Lord.
Praise be to You, O Christ.

Silence for reflection.

Canticle

Silent night, holy night!
All is calm, all is bright.
Round yon virgin, mother and child.
Holy infant so tender and mild,
Sleep in heavenly peace.

Silent night, holy night!
Shepherds quake at the sight.
Glories stream from heaven afar
Heavenly hosts sing Alleluia,
Christ the Savior is born.

Silent night, holy night!
Son of God love's pure light.
Radiant beams from Thy holy face
With dawn of redeeming grace,
Jesus Lord, at Thy birth.

Second Reading of the Gospel

The Holy Gospel of Our Lord Jesus Christ according to John (6:35-40)

Jesus said to them, "I am the bread of life. Whoever comes to me will never be hungry, and whoever believes in me will never be thirsty. But I said to you that you have seen me and yet do not believe. Everything that the Father gives to me will come to me, and anyone who comes to me I will never drive away; for I have come down from heaven, not to do my own will, but the will of him who sent me. And this is the will of him who sent me, that I should lose nothing of all that he has given me, but raise it up on the last day. This is indeed the will of my father, that all who see the Son and believe in him may have eternal life; and I will raise them up on the last day."

The Gospel of the Lord.
Praise be to You, O Christ.

Silence for reflection, homily or reading. Be seated.

[Jesus said he will lose nothing of all that the Father has given him - and that includes you! What are your feelings around this?]

Magnificat

My soul proclaims the greatness of the Lord*
    My spirit rejoices in God my Savior.
You have looked with favor on your humble servant*
    And all generations will call me blessed.
You, O God, have done great things for me*
    And holy is your name.
You have mercy on those who love you*
    From generation to generation.
You have shown the strength of your arm*
    And have scattered the proud in their conceit.
You have cast down the mighty from their thrones*
    And have lifted up the lowly,
You have filled the hungry with good things*
    And the rich you have sent away empty.
You have come to the help of your people*
    For you remembered your promise of mercy.
The promise you made to our forbears*
To Abraham and his children forever.

Lord, O Gracious Light!
Christ, O Perfect Love!
Lord, O Gracious Light!

Hymn   (Silent Night, Holy Night)

III. The Prayers

The Lord be with you.
And also with you.

The Lord's Prayer   *(Stand facing altar)*

Our Father in heaven, hallowed be your name,
    Your kingdom come, your will be done,
    On earth as it is in heaven.
Give us today our daily bread.
Forgive us, as we forgive others.
Save us from the time of trial and deliver us from evil.
For the kingdom, the power, and the glory are yours
    Now and forever. Amen

Collect

Almighty God, you have sent down from heaven the living bread that feeds us eternal life: Grant that our gladness of heart meets some need here in this world so that we may serve you in fullness; through Jesus Christ our Lord, who lives and reigns with you and the Holy Spirit, one God, for evermore. **Amen.**

Additional Prayers may be added here.

May the God of hope fill you with all joy and peace in believing, so that you may abound in hope by the power of the Holy Spirit. **Amen.**

Let us bless the Lord.   **Thanks be to God.**

January 3

MORNING PRAYER

I. Invitatory

The officiant opens with this sentence: (All stand)

Alleluia! To us a child is born! *
Come let us adore him. Alleluia!

O Lord, Open our lips. *
And our mouth shall proclaim Your praise.

Glory to the Father, and to the Son,
and to the Holy Spirit. *
As it was in the beginning, is now,
and will be for ever. Amen.

Psalm

For Jesus Christ our Savior
Was born on Christmas day.

Psalm 48(9-14)

We ponder your steadfast love, O God, *
    in the midst of your temple.
Your name, O God, like your praise, *
    reaches to the ends of the earth.
Your right hand is filled with victory, *
    Let Mount Zion be glad,
Let the towns of Judah rejoice *
    because you judge fairly.
Walk about Zion, go all around it, *
    count its towers, consider well its ramparts;
Go through its citadels, *
    that you may tell the next generation,
This is God, our God for ever and ever.*
    He will be our guide forever.

Glory to the Father, and to the Son,
and to the Holy Spirit. *
As it was in the beginning, is now,
and will be for ever. Amen.

For Jesus Christ our Savior
Was born on Christmas day.

January 3

II. The Lessons *(Be seated)*

Old Testament Lesson

A reading from the book of Ezekiel (34:11- 16)

Thus says the Lord God, I myself will search for my sheep, and will seek them out. As shepherds seek out their flocks when they are among them, so will I seek out my sheep. I will rescue them from all the places to which they have been scattered on a day of clouds and thick darkness. I will bring them out from the peoples and gather them from the countries, and will bring them into their own land; and I will feed them on the mountains of Israel, by the watercourses, and in all the inhabited parts of the land. I will feed them good pasture, and the mountain heights of Israel shall be their pasture; there they shall lie down in good grazing land, and they shall feed on rich pasture on the mountains of Israel. I myself will be the shepherd of my sheep, and I will make them lie down, says the Lord God. I will seek the lost, and I will bring back the strayed, and I will bind up the injured, and I will strengthen the weak; I will feed them with my justice.

The word of the Lord.

Silence for reflection.

Canticle

God rest you merry, gentlemen,
Let nothing you dismay.
For Jesus Christ our Savior,
Was born on Christmas Day;
To save us all from Satan's power,
When we were gone astray.

From God our heavenly Father,
A blessed angel came.
And unto certain shepherds,
Brought tidings of the same,
How that in Bethlehem was born,
The Son of God by name.

The shepherds at those tidings
Rejoiced much in mind,
And left their flocks a-feeding
in tempest, storm and wind,
And went to Bethlehem away
This blessed Babe to find.

Now to the Lord sing praises,
All you within this place,
And with true love and brotherhood,
Each other now embrace;
This holy tide of Christmas,
Doth bring redeeming grace.

January 3

Reading of the Gospel *(All stand)*

The Holy Gospel of Our Lord Jesus Christ according to Matthew (1:18-24)

Now the birth of Jesus the Messiah took place this way. When his mother Mary had been engaged to Joseph, but before they lived together, she was found to be with child from the Holy Spirit. Her betrothed Joseph, being a righteous man and unwilling to expose her to public disgrace, planned to dismiss her quietly. But just when he had resolved to do this, an angel of the Lord appeared to him in a dream and said, "Joseph, son of David, do not be afraid to take Mary as your wife, for the child conceived in her is from the Holy Spirit. She will bear a son, and you are to name him Jesus, for he will save his people from their sins. All this took place to fulfill what had been spoken by the Lord through the prophet: 'Look, the virgin shall conceive and bear a son, and they shall name him Emmanuel, which means, God is with us.'"

The Gospel of the Lord.
Praise be to You, O Christ.

Silence for reflection, homily or reading. Be seated.

[Each person is a temple of God. He abides in us and we in him. You are one of the sheep that God will once again gather into his pastures.]

Benedictus

Blessed are you O Lord our God*
You have come to your people and set them free.
You have raised up for us a mighty Savior*
Born of the house of your servant David.
Through your holy prophets you promised of old*
That you would save us from our enemies,
From the hands of all who hate us.
You promised to show mercy to our forbears*
And to remember your holy covenant.
This was the oath you swore to our father Abraham*
To set us free from the hands of our enemies,
Free to worship you without fear*
Holy and righteous in your sight all the days of our life.
And you, child, shall be called the prophet of the Most High*
For you will go before the Lord to prepare the way,
To give God's people knowledge of salvation*
Through the forgiveness of their sins.
In the tender compassion of our God*
The dawn from on high shall break upon us.
To shine on those who dwell in darkness and the shadow of death*
And to guide our feet into the way of peace.

Glory to the Father, and to the Son,
and to the Holy Spirit. *
**As it was in the beginning, is now,
and will be for ever. Amen.**

Hymn   (God Rest You Merry, Gentlemen)

January 3

III. The Prayers

The Lord be with you all.
And also with you.

The Lord's Prayer *(Stand facing altar)*

Our Father in heaven, hallowed be your name,
    Your kingdom come, your will be done,
    On earth as it is in heaven.
Give us today our daily bread.
Forgive us, as we forgive others.
Save us from the time of trial and deliver us from evil.
For the kingdom, the power, and the glory are yours
    Now and forever. Amen

Collect

O Great Shepherd of Life, grant that we may always know your presence in our hearts, and let this love come into our thoughts, words and deeds, each and every moment we live; through Jesus Christ our Savior, who lives and reigns with you and the Holy Spirit, one God, now and forever. **Amen**.

Additional Prayers may be added here.

The grace of Our Lord Jesus Christ, and the love of God, and the companionship of the Holy Spirit, be in us and those absent from us. **Amen.**

Let us bless the Lord. **Thanks be to God.**

January 3

EVENING PRAYER

I. Invitatory

The officiant opens with this sentence: (All stand)

O God, make speed to save us.
O Lord, make haste to help us.

Glory to the Father, and to the Son,
and to the Holy Spirit. *
As it was in the beginning, is now,
and will be for ever. Amen.

Phos Hilaron

O gracious Light, pure brightness of the ever-living Father in heaven, *
O Jesus Christ, holy and blessed!

Now as we have come to the setting of the sun, and our eyes behold the vesper light, *
We sing your praises, O God: Father, Son and Holy Spirit.

You are worthy at all times to be praised by happy voices, O Son of God, O Giver of life, *
And to be glorified through all the worlds.

Psalm *(from Psalm 72)*

O Come, let us adore him,
Christ the Lord.

Give the king your justice, O God, *
    and your righteousness to a king's son.
May he judge your people with righteousness, *
    and your poor with justice.
May the mountains be prosperous for the people, *
    and the hills, in righteousness.
May he defend the cause of the poor, *
    and give deliverance to the needy.
In his days may righteousness flourish *
    and peace abound, until the moon is no more.
May he have dominion from sea to sea, *
    and from the River to the ends of the earth.
May his foes bow down before him, *
    may all nations give him service.
For he delivers the needy when they call, *
    the poor and those who have no helper.
He has pity on the weak and the needy, *
    and saves the lives of the needy.
From oppression and violence he redeems their life; *
    and precious is their blood in his sight.
Blessed be the Lord, the God of Israel, *
    who alone does wondrous things,
Blessed be his glorious name forever; *
    may his glory fill the whole earth.

Glory to the Father, and to the Son,
and to the Holy Spirit. *
As it was in the beginning, is now,
and will be for ever. Amen.

O Come, let us adore him,
Christ the Lord.

II. The Lessons *(Be seated)*

Old Testament Lesson

A reading from the Book of Isaiah (62:8-12)

The Lord has sworn by his right hand and by his mighty arm: I will not again give your grain to be food for your enemies, and foreigners shall not drink the wine for which you have labored; but those who garner it shall eat it and praise the Lord, and those who gather it shall drink it in my holy courts. Go through the gates, prepare the way for the people; build up the highway, clear it of stones, lift up an ensign over the peoples. The Lord has proclaimed to the end of the earth: Say to daughter Zion, "See, your salvation comes; his reward is with him, and his recompense before him." They shall be called, "The Holy People, The Redeemed of the Lord"; and you shall be called, "Sought out, a city not forsaken."

The Word of the Lord.

Silence for reflection.

Canticle

O come, all ye faithful,
Joyful and triumphant,
O come ye, O come ye to Bethlehem;
Come and behold him,
Born the King of angels;
O Come, let us adore him, Christ the Lord.

God of God, Light of Light,
Lo! he abhors not the Virgin's womb:
Very God, Begotten, not created;

Sing, choirs of angels,
Sing in exultation,
Sing, all ye citizens of heaven above;
Glory to God In the highest;

See how the shepherds,
Summoned to his cradle,
Leaving their flocks, draw nigh to gaze;
We too will thither
Bend our joyful footsteps;

Yea, Lord, we greet thee,
Born this happy morning;
Jesus, to thee be glory given;
Word of the Father,
Now in flesh appearing.

January 3

Reading of the Gospel *(All stand)*

The Holy Gospel of Our Lord Jesus Christ according to John (10:7-11)

So again Jesus said to them, "Very truly, I tell you, I am the gate for the sheep. All who came before me were thieves and bandits; but the sheep did not listen to them. I am the gate. Whoever enters by me will be saved, and will come in and go out and find pasture. The thief comes only to steal and kill and destroy. I came that they may have life, and have it abundantly. I am the good shepherd. The good shepherd lays down his life for the sheep.

The Gospel of the Lord.
Praise be to You, O Christ.

Silence for reflection, homily or reading. Be seated.

[The Lord is our gateway to the kingdom. He came that we may have life, and have it abundantly. The fullness of life comes when we serve him in this world in a way that uses our unique talents, skills, and interests, whatever they are. What need do you see in the world around you that can be filled with your gladness?]

January 3

Magnificat

My soul proclaims the greatness of the Lord*
    My spirit rejoices in God my Savior.
You have looked with favor on your humble servant*
    And all generations will call me blessed.
You, O God, have done great things for me*
    And holy is your name.
You have mercy on those who love you*
    From generation to generation.
You have shown the strength of your arm*
    And have scattered the proud in their conceit.
You have cast down the mighty from their thrones*
    And have lifted up the lowly,
You have filled the hungry with good things*
    And the rich you have sent away empty.
You have come to the help of your people*
    For you remembered your promise of mercy.
The promise you made to our forbears*
To Abraham and his children forever.

Lord, O Gracious Light!
Christ, O Perfect Love!
Lord, O Gracious Light!

Blessed be the Lord, the God of Israel,
who alone does wondrous things.

Hymn   (O Come, All Ye Faithful)

III. The Prayers

The Lord be with you.
And also with you.

The Lord's Prayer   *(Stand facing altar)*

Our Father in heaven, hallowed be your name,
   Your kingdom come, your will be done,
   On earth as it is in heaven.
Give us today our daily bread.
Forgive us, as we forgive others.
Save us from the time of trial and deliver us from evil.
For the kingdom, the power, and the glory are yours
   Now and forever. Amen

Collect

Almighty and All-loving God, you are the gate through which we go for the fullness of life; show us how we can use the gifts you have given us to meet some need in this world, however small we think it is; through Jesus Christ our Shepherd, who lives and reigns with you and the Holy Spirit, one God, now and forever. **Amen**.

Additional Prayers may be added here.

May the God of hope fill you with all joy and peace in believing, so that you may abound in hope by the power of the Holy Spirit. **Amen.**

Let us bless the Lord.   **Thanks be to God.**

January 4

MORNING PRAYER

I. Invitatory

The officiant opens with this sentence: (All stand)

Alleluia! To us a child is born! *
Come let us adore him. Alleluia!

O Lord, Open our lips. *
And our mouth shall proclaim Your praise.

Glory to the Father, and to the Son,
and to the Holy Spirit. *
As it was in the beginning, is now,
and will be for ever. Amen.

Psalm

Hark! the herald angels sing
Glory to the new-born King!

Psalm 87

On the holy mountain stands the city he founded; *
    the Lord loves the gates of Zion
More than all the dwellings of Jacob. *
    Glorious things are spoken of you, O city of God.
Among those who know me I mention Rahab and Babylon;*
    Philistia, too, and Tyre, with Ethiopia
"This one was born there," they say. *
    And of Zion it shall be said,
"This one and that one were born in it"; *
    For the Most High himself will establish it.
The Lord records, as he registers the peoples, *
    "This one was born there."
Singers and dancers alike say, *
    "All my living waters are in you."

Glory to the Father, and to the Son,
and to the Holy Spirit. *
As it was in the beginning, is now,
and will be for ever. Amen.

Hark! the herald angels sing
Glory to the new-born King!

January 4

II. The Lessons *(Be seated)*

Old Testament Lesson

A reading from the book of Isaiah (61:10-11)

I will greatly rejoice in the Lord, my whole being shall exult in my God; for he has clothed me with the garments of salvation, he has covered me with the robe of righteousness, as a bridegroom decks himself with a garland, and as a bride adorns herself with her jewels. For as the earth brings forth its shoots, and as a garden causes what is sown in it to spring up, so the Lord God will cause righteousness and praise to spring up before the nations.

The word of the Lord.

Silence for reflection.

Canticle

Hark! the herald angels sing
Glory to the new-born King!
Peace on earth and mercy mild,
God and sinners reconciled!
Joyful, all ye nations, rise,
Join the triumph of the skies;
With the angelic host proclaim
Christ is born in Bethlehem!

Christ, by highest heaven adored;
Christ, the everlasting Lord;
Late in time behold Him come,
Offspring of the Virgin's womb.
Veiled in flesh the Godhead see;
Hail, the incarnate Deity,
Pleased as man with man to dwell;
Jesus, our Emmanuel!

Mild He lays His glory by,
Born that man no more may die,
Born to raise the sons of earth,
Born to give them second birth.
Risen with healing in His wings,
Light and life to all He brings,
Hail, the Son of Righteousness!
Hail, the heaven-born Prince of Peace!

Come, Desire of nations come,
Fix in us Thy humble home;
Rise, the Woman's conquering Seed,
Bruise in us the Serpent's head.
Adam's likeness now efface:
Stamp Thine image in its place;
Second Adam, from above,
Reinstate us in Thy love.
Hark! the herald angels sing
Glory to the new-born King!

January 4

New Testament Lesson

Reading of the Gospel *(All stand)*

The Holy Gospel of Our Lord Jesus Christ according to Luke (1:26-33)

The angel Gabriel was sent by God to a town in Galilee called Nazareth, to a virgin engaged to a man whose name was Joseph, of the house of David. The virgin's name was Mary. And the angel said to her, "Greetings, favored one! The Lord is with you." But she was much perplexed by his words, so the angel said to her, "Do not be afraid, Mary, for you have found favor with God. And now, you will conceive in your womb and bear a son, and you will name him Jesus. He will be great, and will be called the Son of the Most High, and the Lord God will give to him the throne of his ancestor David. He will reign over the house of Jacob forever, and of his kingdom there shall be no end."

The Gospel of the Lord.
Praise be to You, O Christ.

Silence for reflection, homily or reading. Be seated.

[When we do the will of God, we must remember that God is with us, too, as the angel promised Mary. That doesn't mean the road ahead will be smooth, but it does mean that ultimately all will be well.]

Benedictus

Blessed are you O Lord our God*
You have come to your people and set them free.
You have raised up for us a mighty Savior*
Born of the house of your servant David.
Through your holy prophets you promised of old*
That you would save us from our enemies,
From the hands of all who hate us.
You promised to show mercy to our forbears*
And to remember your holy covenant.
This was the oath you swore to our father Abraham*
To set us free from the hands of our enemies,
Free to worship you without fear*
Holy and righteous in your sight all the days of our life.
And you, child, shall be called the prophet of the Most High*
For you will go before the Lord to prepare the way,
To give God's people knowledge of salvation*
Through the forgiveness of their sins.
In the tender compassion of our God*
The dawn from on high shall break upon us.
To shine on those who dwell in darkness and the shadow of death*
And to guide our feet into the way of peace.

Glory to the Father, and to the Son,
and to the Holy Spirit. *
**As it was in the beginning, is now,
and will be for ever. Amen.**

Hymn   (Hark! The Herald Angels Sing)

III. The Prayers

The Lord be with you all.
And also with you.

The Lord's Prayer *(Stand facing altar)*

Our Father in heaven, hallowed be your name,
    Your kingdom come, your will be done,
    On earth as it is in heaven.
Give us today our daily bread.
Forgive us, as we forgive others.
Save us from the time of trial and deliver us from evil.
For the kingdom, the power, and the glory are yours
    Now and forever. Amen

Collect

Our Father Most High, we thank you for the gift of Christ; Grant that we allow him to enter and remain in our hearts as we move through life, moment by moment, through Jesus Christ our Lord, who lives and reigns with you and the Holy Spirit, one God, for ever and ever. **Amen.**

Additional Prayers may be added here.

The grace of Our Lord Jesus Christ, and the love of God, and the companionship of the Holy Spirit, be in us and those absent from us.   **Amen.**

Let us bless the Lord.   **Thanks be to God.**

EVENING PRAYER

I. Invitatory

The officiant opens with this sentence: (All stand)

O God, make speed to save us.
O Lord, make haste to help us.

Glory to the Father, and to the Son,
and to the Holy Spirit. *
**As it was in the beginning, is now,
and will be for ever. Amen.**

Phos Hilaron

O gracious Light, pure brightness of the ever-living Father in heaven, *
O Jesus Christ, holy and blessed!

Now as we have come to the setting of the sun, and our eyes behold the vesper light, *
We sing your praises, O God: Father, Son and Holy Spirit.

You are worthy at all times to be praised by happy voices, O Son of God, O Giver of life, *
And to be glorified through all the worlds.

January 4

Psalm *from Psalm 89*

Come to Bethlehem and see,
Him whose birth the angels sing.

I will sing of your steadfast love,
O Lord, forever; *
    with my mouth I will proclaim your
    faithfulness to all generations.
I declare that your steadfast love
is established forever; *
    your faithfulness is as firm as the heavens.
You said, "I have made a covenant with my
chosen one, *
    I have sworn to my servant David:
I will establish your descendants forever, *
    and build your throne for all generations."
Let the heavens praise your wonders, O Lord, *
    your faithfulness in the assembly of the holy ones.
For who in the skies can compare to the Lord? *
    Who among the heavenly beings is like the Lord?
I have set the crown on one who is mighty, *
    I have exalted one chosen from the people.
I have found my servant David; *
    with my holy oil I have anointed him.
My hand shall always remain with him; *
    my arm also shall strengthen him.
The enemy shall not outwit him, *
    the wicked shall not humble him.
My faithfulness and steadfast love shall be with him; *
    and in my name he shall be exalted.
I will make him the firstborn, *
    the highest of the kings of the earth.
Forever I will keep my steadfast love for him, *
    and my covenant with him will stand firm.

Glory to the Father, and to the Son,
and to the Holy Spirit. *
**As it was in the beginning, is now,
and will be for ever. Amen.**

Come to Bethlehem and see,
Him whose birth the angels sing.

II. The Lessons *(Be seated)*

Old Testament Lesson

A reading from the Book of Isaiah (55:1-5)

Everyone who thirsts, come to the waters; and you that have no money, come, buy and eat! Come, buy wine and milk without money and without price. Why do you spend your money for that which is not bread, and your labor for that which does not satisfy? Listen to me carefully, and eat what is good, and delight yourselves in rich food. Incline your ear, and come to me; listen, so that you may live. I will make with you an everlasting covenant, my steadfast, sure love for David. See, I made him a witness to the peoples, a leader and commander for the peoples. See, you shall call nations that you do not know, and nations that do not know you shall run to you, because of the Lord your God, the Holy One of Israel, for he has glorified you.

The Word of the Lord.

Silence for reflection.

Canticle

Angels we have heard on high
Sweetly singing o'er the plains,
And the mountains in reply
Echoing their joyous strains.

Shepherds, why this jubilee?
Why your joyous strains prolong?
What the gladsome tidings be
Which inspire your heavenly song?

Come to Bethlehem and see
Him whose birth the angels sing;
Come, adore on bended knee,
Christ the Lord, the newborn King.

See Him in a manger laid,
Whom the choirs of angels praise;
Mary, Joseph, lend your aid,
While our hearts in love we raise.
Gloria, in excelsis Deo!

January 4

Reading of the Gospel *(All stand)*

The Holy Gospel of Our Lord Jesus Christ according to John (14:1-7)

"Do not let your hearts be troubled. Believe in God, believe also in me. In my Father's house there are many dwelling places. If it were not so, would I have told you that I go to prepare a place for you? And if I go and prepare a place for you, I will come again and will take you to myself, so that where I am, there you may be also. And you know the way to the place where I am going." Thomas said to him, "Lord, we do not know where you are going. How can we know the way?" Jesus said to him, "I am the way, and the truth, and the life. No one comes to the Father except through me. If you know me, you will know my Father also. From now on you do know him and have seen him."

The Gospel of the Lord.
Praise be to You, O Christ.

Silence for reflection, homily or reading. Be seated.

[Isaiah asks, "Why do you spend your money for that which is not bread, and your labor for that which does not satisfy?" Are you living the life that God wants you to live, using the special gifts, talents and interests he gave you?]

January 4

Magnificat

My soul proclaims the greatness of the Lord*
　　My spirit rejoices in God my Savior.
You have looked with favor on your humble servant*
　　And all generations will call me blessed.
You, O God, have done great things for me*
　　And holy is your name.
You have mercy on those who love you*
　　From generation to generation.
You have shown the strength of your arm*
　　And have scattered the proud in their conceit.
You have cast down the mighty from their thrones*
　　And have lifted up the lowly,
You have filled the hungry with good things*
　　And the rich you have sent away empty.
You have come to the help of your people*
　　For you remembered your promise of mercy.
The promise you made to our forbears*
To Abraham and his children forever.

Lord, O Gracious Light!
Christ, O Perfect Love!
Lord, O Gracious Light!

Hymn　　(Angels We Have Heard on High)

January 4

III. The Prayers

The Lord be with you.
And also with you.

The Lord's Prayer *(Stand facing altar)*

Our Father in heaven, hallowed be your name,
    Your kingdom come, your will be done,
    On earth as it is in heaven.
Give us today our daily bread.
Forgive us, as we forgive others.
Save us from the time of trial and deliver us from evil.
For the kingdom, the power, and the glory are yours
    Now and forever. Amen

Collect

Heavenly Father, you gave us unique gifts to be used in your service that will bring us happiness; help us to understand the way, the truth, and the life we are supposed to live through Jesus Christ our Redeemer, who lives and reigns with you and the Holy Spirit, one God, for ever and ever. **Amen.**

Additional Prayers may be added here.

May the God of hope fill you with all joy and peace in believing, so that you may abound in hope by the power of the Holy Spirit. **Amen.**

Let us bless the Lord.   **Thanks be to God.**

January 5
Eve of Epiphany

MORNING PRAYER

I. Invitatory

The officiant opens with this sentence: (All stand)

Alleluia! To us a child is born! *
Come let us adore him. Alleluia!

O Lord, Open our lips. *
And our mouth shall proclaim Your praise.

Glory to the Father, and to the Son,
and to the Holy Spirit. *
**As it was in the beginning, is now,
and will be for ever. Amen.**

January 5

Psalm

I love thee, Lord Jesus!
Stay by my side.

Psalm 100

Make a joyful noise to the Lord, all the earth.
Worship the Lord with gladness; *
    come into his presence with singing.
Know that the Lord is God. It is he that made us,
and we are his. *
    We are his people, and the sheep of his pasture.
Enter into his gates with thanksgiving, *
    and his courts with praise.
Give thanks to him, bless his name. *
    For the Lord is good;
His steadfast loves endures forever, *
    and his faithfulness to all generations.

Glory to the Father, and to the Son,
and to the Holy Spirit. *
**As it was in the beginning, is now,
and will be for ever. Amen.**

I love thee, Lord Jesus!
Stay by my side.

January 5

II. The Lessons *(Be seated)*

Old Testament Lesson

A reading from the book of Isaiah (from Chapter 35)

The wilderness and the dry land shall be glad, the desert shall rejoice and blossom; like the crocus it shall blossom abundantly, and rejoice with joy and singing. They shall see the glory of the Lord, the majesty of our God. Strengthen the weak hands, and make firm the feeble knees. Say to those who are of a fearful heart, "Be strong, do not fear! Here is your God. He will come with justice and save you." Then the eyes of the blind shall be opened, and the ears of the deaf unstopped; then the lame shall leap like deer, and the tongue of the speechless sing for joy. For waters shall break forth in the wilderness, and streams in the desert; the burning sand shall become a pool, and the thirsty grounds springs of water. A highway shall be there, and it shall be called the Holy Way. And the ransomed of the Lord shall return, and come to Zion with singing.

The word of the Lord.

Silence for reflection.

January 5

Canticle

Away in a manger, no crib for a bed,
The little Lord Jesus laid down his sweet head.
The stars in the bright sky looked down where he lay,
The little Lord Jesus asleep on the hay.

The cattle are lowing, the baby awakes,
But little Lord Jesus no crying he makes.
I love thee, Lord Jesus! Look down from the sky,
And stay by my side until morning is nigh.

Be near me Lord Jesus
I ask thee to stay.
Close by me forever,
And love me I pray.

Bless all the dear children,
In thy tender care.
And take them to heaven,
To be with thee there.

January 5

New Testament Lesson

A reading from the Book of 1 Corinthians (from Chapter 12)

Now concerning spiritual gifts, brothers and sisters, I do not want you to be uninformed. There are varieties of gifts, but the same Spirit; and there are varieties of services, but the same Lord; and there are varieties of activities, but it is the same God who activates all of them in everyone. To each is given the manifestation of the Spirit for the common good. All these are activated by one and the same Spirit, who allots to each one individually just as the Spirit chooses. For as the body is one and has many members, and all the members of the body, though many, are one body, so it is with Christ. For in the one Spirit we were all baptized into one body, and we were all made to drink of one Spirit.

The word of the Lord.

Silence for reflection, homily or reading

[You, too, are part of Christ's body, having been received by him, and been given special, unique gifts to be used in his service in your life through Jesus Christ. When the gladness of your heart meets some worldly need, you are living the fullest and glorifying God.]

January 5

Benedictus

Blessed are you O Lord our God*
You have come to your people and set them free.
You have raised up for us a mighty Savior*
Born of the house of your servant David.
Through your holy prophets you promised of old*
That you would save us from our enemies,
From the hands of all who hate us.
You promised to show mercy to our forbears*
And to remember your holy covenant.
This was the oath you swore to our father Abraham*
To set us free from the hands of our enemies,
Free to worship you without fear*
Holy and righteous in your sight all the days of our life.
And you, child, shall be called the prophet of the Most High*
For you will go before the Lord to prepare the way,
To give God's people knowledge of salvation*
Through the forgiveness of their sins.
In the tender compassion of our God*
The dawn from on high shall break upon us.
To shine on those who dwell in darkness and the shadow of death*
And to guide our feet into the way of peace.

Glory to the Father, and to the Son,
and to the Holy Spirit. *
As it was in the beginning, is now,
and will be for ever. Amen.

Hymn (Away in a Manger)

January 5

III. The Prayers

The Lord be with you all.
And also with you.

The Lord's Prayer *(Stand facing altar)*

Our Father in heaven, hallowed be your name,
> Your kingdom come, your will be done,
> On earth as it is in heaven.
Give us today our daily bread.
Forgive us, as we forgive others.
Save us from the time of trial and deliver us from evil.
For the kingdom, the power, and the glory are yours
> Now and forever. Amen

Collect

O Blessed Father, who works through the Holy Spirit in our lives; teach us what gifts you have given us, and help us to appreciate them regardless of how they are valued in mankind's world; through Jesus Christ our Lord, who lives and reigns with you and the Holy Spirit, one God, for ever and ever. **Amen.**

Additional Prayers may be added here.

The grace of Our Lord Jesus Christ, and the love of God, and the companionship of the Holy Spirit, be in us and those absent from us.   **Amen.**

Let us bless the Lord.   **Thanks be to God.**

January 5

EVENING PRAYER

I. Invitatory

The officiant opens with this sentence: (All stand)

O God, make speed to save us.
O Lord, make haste to help us.

Glory to the Father, and to the Son,
and to the Holy Spirit. *
**As it was in the beginning, is now,
and will be for ever. Amen.**

Phos Hilaron

O gracious Light, pure brightness of the ever-living Father
in heaven, *
O Jesus Christ, holy and blessed!

Now as we have come to the setting of the sun, and our eyes
behold the vesper light, *
**We sing your praises, O God: Father, Son and Holy
Spirit.**

You are worthy at all times to be praised by happy voices,
O Son of God, O Giver of life, *
And to be glorified through all the worlds.

Psalm *Psalm 29*

King forever, Ceasing never
Over us all to reign.

Ascribe to the Lord, O heavenly beings, *
    ascribe to the Lord glory and strength.
Ascribe to the Lord the glory of his name; *
    worship the Lord in holy splendor.
The voice of the Lord is over the waters; *
    the God of glory thunders over mighty waters.
The voice of the Lord is powerful; *
    the voice of the Lord is full of majesty.
The voice of the Lord breaks the cedars; *
    the Lord breaks the cedars of Lebanon.
He makes Lebanon skip like a calf, *
    and Sirion like a young wild ox.
The voice of the Lord flashes forth flames of fire.
    The voice of the Lord shakes the wilderness.
The voice of the Lord causes oaks to whirl, *
    and can strip the forests bare;
And in his temple all say, "Glory!" *
    The Lord sits enthroned as king forever.
May the Lord give strength to his people! *
    May the Lord bless his people with peace.

Glory to the Father, and to the Son,
and to the Holy Spirit. *
As it was in the beginning, is now,
and will be for ever. Amen.

King forever, Ceasing never
Over us all to reign.

January 5

II. The Lessons *(Be seated)*

Old Testament Lesson

A reading from the Book of Isaiah (from Chapter 66)

For I know their works and their thoughts, and I am coming to gather all nations and tongues; and they shall come and shall see my glory, and I will set a sign among them. For as the new heavens and the new earth, which I will make, shall remain before me, says the Lord; so shall your descendants and your name remain. From new moon to new moon, and from Sabbath to Sabbath, all flesh shall come to worship before me, says the Lord.

The Word of the Lord.

Silence for reflection.

Canticle

We three kings of Orient are
Bearing gifts, we traverse afar.
Field and fountain, moor and mountain,
Following yonder star.

Born a King on Bethlehem plain,
Gold I bring to crown Him again,
King forever, Ceasing never
Over us all to reign.

Frankincense to offer have I;
Incense owns a Deity nigh:
Prayer and praising
All men raising,
Worship Him God on high.

Myrrh is mine; it's bitter perfume;
Breathes a life of gathering gloom:
Sorrowing, sighing,
Bleeding, dying,
Sealed in the stone-cold tomb.

Glorious now behold Him arise,
King and God and sacrifice.
Heaven sings Halleluiah;
Hallelujah the earth replies.

O star of wonder, star of night,
Star with royal beauty bright,
Westward leading, still proceeding,
Guide us to Thy perfect light.

January 5

Reading of the Gospel *(All stand)*

The Holy Gospel of Our Lord Jesus Christ according to Matthew (2:7-12)

Then Herod secretly called for the wise men and learned from them the exact time when the star had appeared. Then he sent them to Bethlehem, saying, "Go and search diligently for the child; and when you have found him, bring me word so that I may also go and pay him homage." When they had heard the king, they set out; and there, ahead of them, went the star that they had seen at its rising, until it stopped over the place where the child was. When they saw that the star had stopped, they were overwhelmed with joy. On entering the house, they saw the child with Mary his mother; and they knelt down and paid him homage. Then, opening their treasure chests, they offered him gifts of gold, frankincense and myrrh. And having been warned in a dream not to return to Herod, they left for their own country by another road.

The Gospel of the Lord.
Praise be to You, O Christ.

Silence for reflection, homily or reading. Be seated.

[Sometimes we may have to take a different road from the one we planned. How can you be ready for this?]

Magnificat

My soul proclaims the greatness of the Lord*
    My spirit rejoices in God my Savior.
You have looked with favor on your humble servant*
    And all generations will call me blessed.
You, O God, have done great things for me*
    And holy is your name.
You have mercy on those who love you*
    From generation to generation.
You have shown the strength of your arm*
    And have scattered the proud in their conceit.
You have cast down the mighty from their thrones*
    And have lifted up the lowly,
You have filled the hungry with good things*
    And the rich you have sent away empty.
You have come to the help of your people*
    For you remembered your promise of mercy.
The promise you made to our forbears*
To Abraham and his children forever.

Lord, O Gracious Light!
Christ, O Perfect Love!
Lord, O Gracious Light!

Hymn   (We Three Kings of Orient Are)

III. The Prayers

The Lord be with you.
And also with you.

The Lord's Prayer *(Stand facing altar)*

Our Father in heaven, hallowed be your name,
    Your kingdom come, your will be done,
    On earth as it is in heaven.
Give us today our daily bread.
Forgive us, as we forgive others.
Save us from the time of trial and deliver us from evil.
For the kingdom, the power, and the glory are yours
    Now and forever. Amen

Collect

Almighty and ever living God, we thank you for the gifts of Christmas; you sent your Son to teach us, and guide us, and redeem us from darkness; Grant that his Light continues to be with us throughout the year; through Jesus Christ our Lord, who lives and reigns with you and the Holy Spirit, one God, for ever and ever. **Amen.**

Additional Prayers may be added here.

May the God of hope fill you with all joy and peace in believing, so that you may abound in hope by the power of the Holy Spirit. **Amen.**

Let us bless the Lord. **Thanks be to God.**

About the Author

Br Daniel-Joseph Schroeder completed his undergraduate studies in Classical Hebrew at the University of Wisconsin-Milwaukee. He is the founder of the Community of the Gospel, a dispersed monastic Episcopal Christian Community which has members across the United States. Brother also has a Master of Science in adult educational psychology and an MBA in finance.

www.communityofthegospel.org

www.ingramcontent.com/pod-product-compliance
Lightning Source LLC
Chambersburg PA
CBHW051947290426
44110CB00015B/2144